The Other Side of the Report Card

The Other Side of the Report Card

Assessing Students' Social, Emotional, and Character Development

Maurice J. Elias

Joseph J. Ferrito

Dominic C. Moceri

Foreword by Timothy Shriver and Mark Greenberg

CORWIN
A SAGE Company

FOR INFORMATION:

Corwin
A SAGE Company
2455 Teller Road
Thousand Oaks, California 91320
(800) 233-9936
www.corwin.com

SAGE Publications Ltd.
1 Oliver's Yard
55 City Road
London EC1Y 1SP
United Kingdom

SAGE Publications India Pvt. Ltd.
B 1/I 1 Mohan Cooperative Industrial Area
Mathura Road, New Delhi 110 044
India

SAGE Publications Asia-Pacific Pte. Ltd.
3 Church Street
#10-04 Samsung Hub
Singapore 049483

Senior Acquisitions Editor: Jessica Allan
Senior Associate Editor: Kimberly Greenberg
Editorial Assistant: Katie Crilley
Production Editor: Amy Schroller
Copy Editor: Jared Leighton
Typesetter: Hurix Systems Pvt. Ltd.
Proofreader: Lawrence W. Baker
Indexer: Nancy Fulton
Cover Designer: Scott Van Atta
Marketing Manager: Jill Margulies

Printed in the United States of America

ISBN 978-1-4833-8667-6

Library of Congress Cataloging-in-Publication Data

Names: Elias, Maurice J., author.

Title: The other side of the report card : assessing students' social, emotional, and character development / Maurice J. Elias, Joseph J. Ferrito, Dominic C. Moceri.

Description: Thousand Oaks, California : Corwin, a SAGE Company, [2016] | Includes bibliographical references and index.

Identifiers: LCCN 2015034875 | ISBN 9781483386676 (pbk. : alk. paper)

Subjects: LCSH: Educational tests and measurements. | Personality development—Evaluation.

Classification: LCC LB3051 .E47 2016 | DDC 371.26—dc23 LC record available at http://lccn.loc.gov/2015034875

This book is printed on acid-free paper.

16 17 18 19 20 10 9 8 7 6 5 4 3 2 1

CONTENTS

Visit the companion website at
http://resources.corwin.com/EliasReportCard
for the following online supplements:

SEL Skill Trajectory, Grades 1–12

Utility: This details SEL skill categories and subcategories and the specific observable behaviors that compose each across the developmental trajectory. This may promote consistency in ratings and help acclimate teachers to rating students in grades they have not previously worked with.

Developmentally Adapted SEL Likert Rating System: Progression by Grade Level

Utility: This shows one way the development of specific, concrete behaviors related to SEL skills can be captured in a series of Likert ratings targeted at various developmental stages and grade ranges.

LIST OF ESSENTIAL TABLES

FOREWORD

The authors of *The Other Side of the Report Card* have written an important yet accessible book. It is steeped in the latest research in the fields of social and emotional learning (SEL) and character education (CE) and they make this research both accessible and actionable to the general reader and specialist alike. It will surely have a significant impact on building consensus for alignment in both of these fast-growing fields.

Most important, this book addresses the most critical issue facing the fields today: assessment. The authors help us understand the central importance of SEL and CE both in motivating children to learn and also in educating them in skills and values that will matter to them throughout their lives. But they do more than stipulate to this importance; they show in practical ways how this importance can influence the essential area of assessment and reporting. By providing both examples of innovative "report cards" as well as step-by-step procedures for a school to create its own assessment process, the authors provide a detailed roadmap for creating new and innovative models of assessment that will align with the Common Core and give teachers and parents new and vital information on student development. This is an area that requires urgent attention if SEL and CE are to make a sustained and sustainable difference to teachers, students, and families, and this book will make a significant difference in driving that hope forward. Readers will come to understand what elements of SEL and CE can be assessed quantitatively and which are better left to more open-ended forms of reporting. They will be able to see how new strategies for assessment can be applied to local schools and districts.

This book will go a long way to defining a new consensus on how to measure the things that matter most. There is hardly a more pressing issue in education today.

—*Timothy P. Shriver, PhD,*
Cofounder of CASEL

—*Mark T. Greenberg, PhD,*
Bennett Chair of Prevention Research,
Penn State University

ACKNOWLEDGMENTS

Support for the creation of this Guide came in part from funding from the Collaborative for Academic, Social, and Emotional Learning (CASEL), through a grant from the NoVo Foundation.

Foremost, we wish to acknowledge that our project was funded in part by a grant from CASEL, from a larger grant they received from the NoVo Foundation. In particular, Roger Weissberg, Mark Greenberg, and Paul Goren of CASEL lent immeasurable support at various points in the project. We also recognize our intellectual debts to those individuals who founded the fields of social-emotional and character development. They are too many to name, but we are clear that we stand on the shoulders of many visionaries and persistent advocates for promoting the well-being of children and an inspiring, supportive, safe school culture and climate.

We also have some particular personal acknowledgments that we would like to make. We have been blessed with many supportive family members, colleagues, and friends who have influenced and encouraged our work. Joseph (JJ) would like to thank his mother, father, sister, and brother, who have continually served as role models, who broadened his perspective on himself and others. It is JJ's hope that this form of growth will be promoted for all children through this Guide. Dominic would like to thank his wife, sister, mother, father, and grandparents for being strong supporters of his education and for always providing him with love and emotional support. Maurice would like to recognize the enduring influence and continuing presence of beloved mentors, Joe Zins, Irv Sigel, Tom Schuyler, Jackie Norris, Larry Leverett, Ed Dunkelblau, and Tim Shriver. He would also like to thank a large group of dedicated and talented undergraduate and graduate students at Rutgers who have been such marvelous collaborators on this and related projects, especially Jazmin Reyes, Gwyne White, Cesalie Stepney, Danielle Hatchimonji, and Arielle Linsky.

Finally, we are grateful to our previously anonymous reviewers and to our Corwin editorial team for sharp insights, patient encouragement, and working in the spirit of continuous improvement in the interest of children.

PUBLISHER'S ACKNOWLEDGMENTS

Corwin would like to thank the following individuals for their editorial insight and guidance:

Deborah Alexander
Educational Consultant
Tennessee Technological University
Cookeville, TN

Rose-Marie Botting
Retired Elementary School Teacher
Science Curriculum Specialist

Tonia Guidry
Teacher
Golden Meadow Middle School
Golden Meadow, LA

Charles L. Lowery
Assistant Professor of Educational Studies
Ohio University
Athens, OH

Neil MacNeill
Head Master
Ellenbrook Independent Primary School
Western Australia, Australia

Laura Mahler
Teacher, Educational Consultant
Clarkston Community Schools
Clarkston, MI

Phyllis Ness
K–5 Literacy Specialist and Subject Area
    Coordinator
Clarkston Community Schools
Clarkston, MI

Pamela L. Opel
Teacher, Intervention Specialist
Gulfport School District
Gulfport, MS

Patricia Palmer
Sixth-Grade Teacher, NBCT
Wynford School
Bucyrus, OH

ABOUT THE AUTHORS

 **Maurice J. Elias, PhD,** is Professor, Psychology Department, Rutgers University, Director of the Rutgers Social-Emotional Learning Lab, and Academic Director of The Collaborative Center for Community-Based Research and Service at Rutgers. He is Past President of the Society for Community Research and Action/Division of Community Psychology (27) of APA and has received the Society for Community Research and Action Distinguished Contribution to Practice and Ethnic Minority Mentoring Awards, as well the Joseph E. Zins Memorial Senior Scholar Award for Social-Emotional Learning from the Collaborative for Academic, Social, and Emotional Learning (CASEL), the John P. McGovern Medal from the American School Health Association, and the Sanford McDonnell Award for Lifetime Achievement in Character Education.

Prof. Elias lectures nationally and internationally to educators and parents about students' emotional intelligence, school success, and social-emotional and character development. Among Dr. Elias's numerous books are the Association for Supervision and Curriculum Development's (ASCD's) *Promoting Social and Emotional Learning: Guidelines for Educators*, the *Social Decision Making/Social Problem Solving* curricula for Grades K–8, the new e-book, *Emotionally Intelligent Parenting*, and a book for young children: *Talking Treasure: Stories to Help Build Emotional Intelligence and Resilience in Young Children* (www.researchpress.com, 2012). He also writes a blog on SEL-related topics for the George Lucas Educational Foundation at www.edutopia.org.

With colleagues at the College of St. Elizabeth, he has developed an online credentialing program for Direct Instruction of Social-Emotional and Character Development (SECD) programs in classroom, small group, and after school settings (sel.rutgers.edu), and for School-Focused Leadership and Coordination of SECD and School Culture and Climate (SELinSchools.org).

Joseph J. Ferrito recently earned his doctoral degree from the Graduate School of Applied and Professional Psychology at Rutgers University. He is a native of Monroe Township, New Jersey and a graduate of Marist College where he majored in psychology. Clinically, Dr. Ferrito trained and worked across levels of care ranging from public schools and in-home services, to residential and inpatient treatment facilities. His clinical work has focused on children, adolescents, and families, particularly those who have been exposed to various traumatic experiences. He completed an APA-accredited internship at Sharp HealthCare in San Diego, California and is currently a post-doctoral fellow at the Audrey Hepburn Children's House at Hackensack University Medical Center in New Jersey.

Throughout his graduate training, Ferrito taught several undergraduate courses and conducted research under the mentorship of Dr. Maurice J. Elias through the Social-Emotional Learning (SEL) Lab at Rutgers University. Developing feasible methods for assessing SEL and related skills in schools has been a focus of this research and this work has generated several publications in various forms. Ferrito hopes to continue this work and combine it with his interest in trauma and resiliency to enhance evidence-based methods of prevention and promotion on a national and international level.

Dominic C. Moceri graduated with his PhD in clinical psychology from Rutgers, The State University of New Jersey. While at Rutgers, his research focused on quantifying the dissemination, implementation, sustainability, and scalability of evidence-based practices in schools and other settings. Moceri was co-principal investigator of the initial SEL Report Card Indicator studies, the foundation for this book. Additionally, he was the lead creator of the Schools Implementing Towards Sustainability (SITS) scale, a user-friendly and scalable measure of the system of sustainable implementation framework (Moceri et al., 2012). He received his M.S. in clinical psychology from Rutgers and his B.A. with honors in psychology from the University of Michigan.

Dr. Moceri currently practices cognitive-behavioral therapy and conducts psychological assessments with children, adolescents, and adults in his home state of Michigan. He assesses and treats a wide variety of presenting problems, including anxiety, depression, inattention, hyperactivity, oppositionality, and rage attacks. He specializes in the treatment of obsessive-compulsive disorder, anxiety disorders, and tic disorders using exposure and response prevention and habit reversal training.

Intelligence plus character,
That is the goal of true education.

—Rev. Dr. Martin Luther King Jr.

INTRODUCTION

Educating the mind without educating the heart is not education at all.

—Aristotle

To educate a person in mind and not in morals is to create a menace to society.

—Theodore Roosevelt

Utility: We provide a basic overview of the mission and purpose of this Guide.

Key Takeaway and Reflection Points:

- Educators have long been dedicated to the mission of promoting student success in school and life.

- Student success stems from intellectual and academic prowess in combination with an array of behaviors described by SEL skills and character attributes.

- These types of behaviors have long been recognized by educators as important, as is clear based on the long history of having behavioral feedback provided on the "the other side of the report card."

Educators in schools across the nation collectively interact with millions of students every day. Each student is on a trajectory that will shape and influence the type of citizen he or she will eventually become. After each school day of overflowing responsibilities and endless additional hours of planning, we spend our nights contemplating to what end our hard work is leading our students and how we can reach goals more efficiently. The current educational climate also raises questions about whether our focus on preparing students for academic tests is balanced with preparing them for the tests of life.

Knowing that it is impossible to describe each student's academic life fully, it is therefore desirable to provide the most essential feedback on student progress in school in a realistic way. Report cards are perhaps the most widely used method of feedback, with subject area grades long representing the top priority of schools: academic achievement. Historically, we also have had "the other side of the report card," onto which we have recorded comments relevant to character, motivation, preparation, and more. The presence of these comments is a testament to educators who recognize the essential role of behavior in both achievement and student growth. The gifts of individual students, including their academic abilities, personality, character, and skills of relating and interacting, combine with complexity and emerge and develop inevitably in the school environment. It is intuitive as well as grounded in research that these skills relate to how a student functions both inside and outside of school.

Our report cards frame essential, multiyear conversations between students and teachers, teachers and parents, and parents and students. Some of the most important of these conversations, particularly for parents and guardians who are not as closely attuned to schools' academic rigors, revolve around "the other side of the report card." We must ask ourselves if current comment systems address the behaviors most worth talking about, that is, those most essential to promote and best aligned with our ultimate goal of educating the future citizens of our society.

The Collaborative for Academic, Social, and Emotional Learning (CASEL) has conducted systematic research through collaboration with a multitude of school districts throughout the nation to explore this exact question. Which behaviors are most essential for students to develop and display in order to best learn as they grow into young adults? Through this research, they have found that there are specific social-emotional skills composing five major areas that improve academic achievement, increase positive behaviors (e.g., attitude toward school), and decrease negative behaviors (e.g., bullying and truancy) (see http://www.casel .org/library/2014/1/29/meta-analysis-of-school-based-universal-interventions). Referred to as the CASEL 5, the skill areas are self-awareness, self-management, social awareness, relationship skills, and responsible decision making.

At the same time, Paul Tough, in his influential book *How Children Succeed*, reports on a parallel set of efforts to recognize that aspects of character—such as, responsibility, leadership, caring, and grit—also matter for student success in school and life. Conversations about character also have a place on "the other side of the report card" as they stem from one of the most universal questions parents have when they come into a school to meet with teachers: Is my son or daughter a "good child"? Parallel to the work of CASEL, Character.org has been at the forefront of other educational organizations focusing on the development of students' character. Among the commonly agreed-upon dimensions of character strengths, drawn largely from the work cited by Tough, are grit, gratitude, responsibility, optimism, zest, and temperance (self-control). These dimensions also have been the focus of research illustrating their relevance to academic and life success (see the Resources section following Chapter 8 for research on social-emotional learning [SEL] and character).

This Guide provides educators with the tools and guidance to adapt current report card comment systems to include aspects of social-emotional competencies and character development that they deem most important. The process of schools and/or districts deciding on the specific content and format of "the other side of the report card" is a powerful vehicle for creating greater cohesion and intentionality within school systems. It creates a connection with systematic efforts to build students' social-emotional skills and character as well as opportunities for new and valuable conversations involving educators, students, and parents. Additionally, it fosters the conditions essential for academic success and college, career, and citizenship preparation.

1

IS IT REALISTIC TO INCLUDE SOCIAL-EMOTIONAL SKILLS AND CHARACTER ON REPORT CARDS?

Utility: We provide overviews of social-emotional learning (SEL) and character development (CD) and identify specific behaviors representative of each. A description of the lack of support in research for current comment systems and some key rationales as to why report card comments should be changed are included. This chapter also includes an analysis of driving forces for making changes to comments and an overview of the inefficient nature of current comment systems.

Maximizing Guide Resources: Consider adapting or distributing this part of the Guide for key stakeholders or staff to promote awareness and buy-in.

Key Takeaway and Reflection Points:

- SEL refers to a set of skills. A prominent categorization is the CASEL 5, which includes self-awareness, self-management, social awareness, relationship skills, and responsible decision making (see Table 1.1).

- CD refers to both moral character rooted in virtues (e.g., integrity, justice, and respect) and performance character (e.g., perseverance, optimism, and work ethic) (see Table 1.2).

- Taken together, SEL and CD can be referred to as SECD (social, emotional, and character development), highlighting the overlap and importance of both.

- States and countries are integrating SEL and CD into a variety of mandated programming, including early learning standards and the Common Core and related state standards.

- Current report card comment systems lack research demonstrating their efficacy in promoting student success in school and life.

- Consider the "Driving Forces for Adding SECD to Report Cards" bulleted points. How salient are practical and conceptual advantages for your school or district?

IN THIS CHAPTER

The saying "What is important is what gets assessed" is a bit too simplistic. In fact, the first question should be "What is important?," followed by "How can we assess it?" So the answer to the question that opens the chapter, "Is it realistic to include social-emotional skills and character on report cards?," depends on how important you feel those areas are to your students, fellow educators, school, and community.

If you value data, then you will be reassured that over 200 studies support the significance of the role of social-emotional and character development on student academic outcomes, classroom behavior, attitudes toward school, treatment of other students, and beliefs in their own competences and efficacy (Brown, Corrigan, & Higgins-D'Alessandro, 2012; Durlak, Domitrovich, Weissberg, & Gullotta, 2015; see also www.characterandcitizenship.org).

If you simply love children, believe in the developmental education of the whole child, understand what is necessary for college and career success, or want to prepare students for the tests of life and not just a life of tests, you may also value social-emotional and character development. While much has been written about this area, we want to share our perspective here.

WHAT IS SOCIAL-EMOTIONAL AND CHARACTER DEVELOPMENT?

Simply put, social-emotional and character development represents the convergence of two trends in education, social-emotional learning (SEL) and character education (CE). Both SEL and CE have two flagship organizations, the Collaborative for Academic, Social, and Emotional Learning (CASEL) and Character.org (formerly the Character Education Partnership), and each has a website that is an outstanding source of ongoing information about each perspective, www.casel.org and www.character.org.

SEL refers to a set of skills that are important elements of everyday life and are present and relevant from infancy through old age: recognizing and managing emotions, developing empathy and concern for others, establishing effective relationships in one-on-one and group contexts, making responsible and ethical decisions, and handling challenging situations constructively. These skills allow students to function well in classrooms, in schoolyards, on the bus, during recess, and in after-school programs. They are able to calm themselves when upset, initiate friendships and resolve conflicts respectfully, and make choices that are ethical and safe. Table 1.1 includes the most common definition of SEL mentioned earlier in the introduction, the CASEL 5, with detailed definitions and behavioral examples (see Payton et al., 2008, for additional detail). From even a cursory reading, it should be clear how essential these skills are for virtually everything that occurs in schools, whether in classroom or other contexts, because both the skills and what happens in schools are grounded in interpersonal relationships.

Character has two essential parts: moral character and performance character. Moral character encompasses the knowledge of essential virtues—such as integrity, justice, caring, respect, and citizenship—needed for successful interpersonal relationships,

Table 1.1 The CASEL 5: Definitions and Skills Examples

Self-Awareness	Self-Management	Social Awareness	Relationship Skills	Responsible Decision Making
• Accurately assessing one's feelings, interests, values, and strengths • Maintaining a well grounded sense of self confidence	• Regulating one's emotions to handle stress, control impulses, and persevere in addressing challenges • Expressing emotions appropriately • Setting and monitoring progress toward personal and academic goals	• Being able to take the perspective of and empathize with others • Recognizing and appreciating individual and group similarities and differences • Recognizing and making best use of family, school, and community resources	• Establishing and maintaining healthy and rewarding relationships based on cooperation • Resisting inappropriate social pressure • Preventing, managing, and resolving interpersonal conflict • Seeking help when needed	• Making decisions based on consideration of ethical standards, safety concerns, appropriate social norms, respect for others, and likely consequences of various actions • Applying decision-making skills to academic and social situations • Contributing to the well-being of one's school and community
Skills Examples	*Skills Examples*	*Skills Examples*	*Skills Examples*	*Skills Examples*
• *Emotion recognition* • *Identifying feelings* • *Reflection on how one's behavior supports a caring community* • *Recognizing how emotions make our bodies feel* • *Understanding causes of emotions*	• *Goal setting* • *Self-calming and control* • *Changing emotions* • *Positive self-talk* • *Self-control* • *Appropriate expression of emotions*	• *Considering different points of view* • *Empathy* • *Understanding facial, verbal, and situational cues* • *Accurately assessing intentions* • *Appreciating diversity* • *Treating others fairly and being polite*	• *Communication and listening* • *Demonstrating respect and fairness* • *Being cooperative* • *Initiating positive relationships* • *Conflict resolution* • *Handling criticism* • *Teamwork* • *Inclusion*	• *Cognitive, interpersonal, and group problem solving* • *Flexible thinking* • *Taking responsibility for one's self* • *Evaluating possible consequences, solutions, and outcomes* • *Fairness* • *Participating in group decision making*

ethical conduct, and productive living. Performance character represents the qualities and competencies individuals need to live up to their potential for excellence, including enacting the virtues of moral character. Attributes and skills such as perseverance, optimism, a sound work ethic, emotion regulation, interpersonal and communication skills, and problem solving are all needed to perform in a way that reflects one's moral character in school, after school, vocationally, in higher education, and in the community.

Table 1.2 presents a set of character strengths based on the work of Paul Tough and the KIPP schools cited earlier in the introduction. These strengths are commonly identified as part of positive psychology and often included as part of character education programs. In Table 1.2, the strengths are accompanied by behavioral indicators.

Table 1.2 Character Strengths and Behavioral Indicators	
Zest	• **Approaching life with excitement and energy; feeling alive and activated** • _Example Indicators:_ Actively participates, shows enthusiasm, invigorates others
Self-Control	• **Regulating what one feels and does; being self-disciplined** • _Example Indicators:_ Comes to class prepared; pays attention and resists distractions; remains calm even when criticized or otherwise provoked; keeps temper in check
Gratitude	• **Being aware of and thankful for opportunities that one has and for good things to happen** • _Example Indicators:_ Recognizes what others have done; shows appreciation for others; appreciates and/or shows appreciation for his/her opportunities
Curiosity	• **Taking an interest in experience and learning new things for its own sake; finding things fascinating** • _Example Indicators:_ Is eager to explore new things; asks and answers questions to deepen understanding; actively listens to others; asks appropriate, probing questions
Optimism	• **Expecting the best in the future and working to achieve it** • _Example Indicators:_ Gets over frustrations and setbacks quickly; believes that effort will improve his or her future; can articulate positive future aspirations and connect current actions to those aspirations
Grit	• **Finishing what one starts; completing something despite obstacles; a combination of persistence and resilience** • _Example Indicators:_ Finishes whatever he or she begins; tries very hard even after experiencing failure; works independently with focus, despite distractions
Social Intelligence	• **Being aware of motives and feelings of other people and oneself; ability to reason within large and small groups** • _Example Indicators:_ Able to find solutions during conflicts with others; demonstrates respect for feelings of others; knows when and how to include others

SOURCE: http://www.kipp.org/our-approach/strengths-and-behaviors

As with SEL, whether one looks at the strengths or the indicators, it is hard to imagine a well-functioning school in the absence of appropriate character development on the part of children.

In this Guide, we refer to SEL, CE, and their more descriptive combination, SECD—social-emotional and character development—to integrate these ideas and show that regardless of whether a school chooses to emphasize one or the other, both concepts include a combination of skills and values necessary to prepare students for success in school and life.

WHY SHOULD WE BE CONCERNED ABOUT SEL OR CHARACTER?

SEL and Character Are Connected to Current and Emerging Mandates

More and more states and countries are turning their attention to early learning standards; bullying prevention; alcohol, drug, and tobacco prevention; whole-child education; career and college readiness, and the Common Core and related state standards. In each of these areas, social-emotional and character competencies are essential, as we will elaborate below and in case examples in Chapters 4 and 5. For the Common Core State Standards and those that have been substituted for them, strong social-emotional and cognitive learning skills are required on the part of students. These skills include emotion vocabulary and recognition, careful and accurate listening, self-regulation, persistence, inquiry, teamwork, reflection, nonviolent conflict resolution, and problem solving (http://www.casel.org/state-standards-for-social-and-emotional-learning/).

In addition, states, districts, and schools with some kind of SEL or CE or related mandate are coming under greater pressure to have systematic assessment in these areas. Ideally, these assessments will be closely linked to the SEL or CE approaches being used in their settings. Among the most efficient and effective ways to accomplish this is via existing school report cards.

We Are Already Rating These Areas but Ineffectively

In fact, educators have always been concerned about students' social-emotional and character development. Usually, this has been referred to under general categories of *behavior*, *citizenship*, and *work habits*, but they have long been a focus of educators' concerns and parent–teacher conversations. These have found their way onto report card comment sections as the primary avenue teachers have consistently used for providing feedback to parents and students on behavior. Originally, those comments would be written in open-ended spaces, but in recent years, these spaces have been supplemented and often supplanted by drop-down menus or checklists of comments from which educators choose some that are most applicable. However, most of these comment systems are problematic.

The Inefficient Nature of Current Comment Systems

There is little published research on existing comment systems. Systematic examination by the Rutgers Social-Emotional Learning (SEL) Lab of report cards from twenty-three schools in five districts has supported the findings of Friedman and Frisbie's (1995) study that revealed that comment systems can vary tremendously across schools. Formats range from unstructured space for teachers to write comments to computerized drop-down menus of as many as eighty different possible comments, from which teachers select two per student per subject area per marking period. Many comments examined by our Lab do not identify a specific observable behavior, skill, or skill set. Instead, comments are stated broadly, lacking definition of what exact behavior or behaviors students must display or how consistently they must do so to support a comment. Examples include the following: tries hard but finds the subject difficult; shows improvement; interferes with class progress; needs to seek help; and shows excellence. These dilute or misdirect the potential impact of the feedback and create immense potential for different interpretations of the same comment among teachers, parents, and students.

To maximize educational efforts and prepare students for both academic tasks as well as the tests of life, additional consideration should be given to the immense potential impact of well-designed comment sections. What is realistic will remain the ultimate question for any modification to current practices, as schools continually face pressures to promote academic achievement with limited resources and seemingly endless lists of responsibilities. Addressing behaviors that have systematically been found in research and practice to promote academic success can be done in a feasible way by modifying current report card comment systems.

DRIVING FORCES FOR ADDING SECD TO REPORT CARDS

Any change in educational practice asks many individuals to look at what they are doing and do things differently. This cannot be asked or considered without well-thought-out justification. In that light, consider the following driving forces for making changes:

- Pedagogical requirements of Common Core State Standards and related standards require social-emotional and character competencies.
  - The Common Core has requirements, such as "attending to text complexity and close reading of text," that are in direct contrast to what students experience outside of school. Their text messages are anything but complex, and much of their close reading is focused on picture captions. Indeed, text is often seen as cumbersome for young people. So while they can and should learn about text complexity and close reading, the process of learning will engender inevitable frustrations, for which a range of SECD competencies will be essential for mastery. Perhaps even more explicitly, the Common Core requires students to question one another, give feedback, work in groups effectively, and exhibit curiosity—also part of SECD competencies.
- Teachers already allocate time to assigning report card comments.
  - Three or four times per year, teachers spend time in grading tasks.
- Comments are often the only formal rating made of student behavior.
  - Yet the comment section, as noted earlier, is often not designed with a systematic focus on school or district priorities.
- Report cards already feature a section for comments.
  - By linking SEL and character to comment sections, a built-in assessment and delivery system that is scalable would be established. Bringing in any new instrument would require a fundamental change in the task of reporting on student behavior.
- Finances are already allocated for the production and distribution of report cards.

- More formal measures of SEL would involve the need for resources to be allocated to obtaining and distributing the measures, having "expert" personnel score and interpret them, and developing a separate feedback system so that results could be distributed to parents and students. Report cards are already in place and behavioral indicators focused on SECD can be more efficiently linked to existing school data warehouses and more easily retrieved for reporting purposes than current comment systems.

- Parents and students could receive feedback on student progress toward demonstrating specific skills shown in research and practice to influence academic achievement as well as a number of positive and negative behaviors.
  - As we will discuss in Chapter 6, parent–teacher, parent–student, and student–teacher conversations focused on SECD rest on a far stronger empirical and practical base than conversations based on the current comment system ratings.

- Student progress toward skill development can be tracked in a meaningful way on an individual, school, and district level.
  - SEL, in particular, calls for strong developmental articulation. This will lead to grade level differentiation in indicators that can, in turn, be linked to age-appropriate interventions. Individual data can be examined to look at a student's progress within a universal (e.g., whole school) or Tier 2 (i.e., more targeted to specific student groups) intervention. Classroom, school, and district data can be looked at to evaluate programs or approaches brought in for SECD improvement.

- Ratings of SEL skills and character can be used as early indicators of students at risk or who may be able to serve as positive role models and resources for their peers.
  - Criteria can be developed to identify students who are consistently not functioning at grade or age level expectations. This can trigger mainstream classroom-based and/or Tier 2 interventions sooner than might otherwise occur because the indicators are directly tied to best-practice intervention approaches. Relatedly, students who are consistently above grade or age level can be models and buddies for students who need skill development.

- SEL and character ratings present a natural opportunity for emphasizing positive behaviors.
  - In an age of accountability, there can be a tendency to focus on the negative—to point out what children are not doing well. SEL and character ratings allow for positive conversations to take place through both the framing and focus of well-constructed indicators.

SUMMARY

Teacher comments have long been provided alongside academic grades to portray each individual student's academic school life in a way that recognizes the essential role of many abilities and competencies in academic performance and potential. Experts are increasingly clear that judgments of individuals' success in most life areas includes not only intellectual prowess but their interpersonal performance. We have all served on committees with colleagues who are extremely smart but not productive members of the team; indeed, their actions often impede the collective work. Educators in the field are recognizing the convergence of the need to promote skills essential for learning and the opportunity to provide feedback on these skills through report card comments. In the world into which our students will enter as adults, there can be no *either-or* of academic or social-emotional and character competencies. Students require *both-and*. Therefore, feedback about students in schools must incorporate both aspects, systematically and carefully.

2

METHODS CURRENTLY IN PRACTICE

Yours and Others'

Utility: With a sense of what is encompassed in SEL and character development, some of the driving forces behind the need to provide feedback on these behaviors, and how report card comment sections offer a feasible and logical avenue to do so, we take a look at some brief examples of adapted comment sections from several schools. This chapter provides a sample set of "typical" report card comments and shows several case examples to demonstrate how schools and districts are using a variety of methods to adapt comment sections in ways that align with current programming and enhance the specificity and poignancy of individual comments. Reviewing various examples may illuminate benefits of adaptation and identify a style or combination of styles best suited for your district or school. (More comprehensive examples are included later in the Guide, along with guided exercises to analyze your current report card comment system.)

Maximizing Guide Resources: Consider using one or more of the brief examples from this chapter as a way to show how comments can be more behaviorally specific and rooted in SEL and/or CD as well as to convey how this process is flexible and customizable. Also, consider distributing one or more of the exercises to key stakeholders to demonstrate the need for adapting current comment systems and/or to task force members (e.g., school and district leadership teams; see Chapters 3 and 4) to highlight specific comments in need of revision or potential behaviors to emphasize.

Key Takeaway and Reflection Points:

* There are many ways to adapt report card comment sections.

* Decisions on how or what to adapt should be based on multiple factors, including existing programming, school and community priorities and culture, and feasibility (see Chapters 3, 4, and 5).

* Do any of the example approaches seem to have potential in your district? Check to see what resources in this Guide may provide further insight into that process by looking at the in-text references, table of contents, or process overview to see if and where case studies, additional example formats, or other supporting materials are located in this text.

* Exercises at the end of this chapter highlight what is currently being emphasized in your comment section. How might you want this emphasis to shift to better represent the values and principles of your school or district? Keep this in mind moving forward.

We noted in Chapter 1 that as the Common Core State Standards or other sets of statewide standards move toward widespread implementation, there is growing recognition that proper implementation of new standards requires strong social-emotional and cognitive learning skills on the part of students. For many schools and districts, a careful look at current report card comments is an essential first step. In working with schools, we have often asked, "How and when did you establish the comment section in your report card?" This has led to fascinating historic, sometimes archeological, quests as most schools had no clear rationale for why and how their comment sections were in their current form. Some schools said they simply purchased them as part of packages with electronic report card providers or data warehouses. Virtually none of the schools with whom we have worked have been able to use systematic, overall, data-driven feedback from their current comment systems to guide discipline or other policies or for evaluating the effectiveness of programs on students.

Several exercises are included in this Guide to help schools examine their current comment sections. There is great value in this analysis and subsequent intentional modification with regard to both the content, wording, and rating formats for the comments. Clarity about preferred practices then opens the door for successful integration of SEL and/or character, as discussed in Chapters 4 and 5.

The following are examples of current rating systems and item wordings being used in schools now, to add perspective and points of comparison. Curious how your report cards might compare or relate to some of these adaptations? At the end of this chapter, Table 2.4 provides some brief exercises to assist in providing a snapshot of what your current comment section structure looks like and how it relates to SEL and character.

EXAMPLES OF CURRENT REPORT CARD MODIFICATIONS: RUBRIC AND LIKERT RATING SYSTEMS

- Table 2.1 provides a list of typical report card comments to serve as a point of comparison. Many districts use comments similar to these as the primary source of behavior feedback to parents.
- Below, examples are provided of how report cards that initially featured typical comments such as these are being adapted using both rubric and Likert rating systems of SEL skills. The first three examples are the product of collaboration between the SEL Lab at Rutgers University and school districts in New Jersey. Each example provides a brief look at different approaches to include feedback on SEL and character.
  - In the "Example From an Elementary School in Central New Jersey," a Likert rating section was added to the report card, rather than making any changes to traditional comments. Likert items were selected by administrators and teachers to reflect the core skills of an SEL curriculum they implemented.

Table 2.1 Typical Report Card Comments

Typical Report Card Comments	
Positive	**Negative**
• Brings material to class daily • Follows directions and rules well • Presents work neatly • Completes homework regularly • Completes class work regularly • Participates well in class discussions • Works well in a group • Works well independently • Demonstrates continuous effort • Demonstrates a positive attitude • Shows improved behavior	• Not prepared for class • Does not follow directions and rules well • Work not presented neatly • Homework not completed regularly • Does not complete class work • Lack of participation in class discussions and group activities • Needs to improve test scores • Does not work independently • Needs to pay closer attention in class • Lack of continuous effort • Does not complete projects on time • Disrespectful to others

o The "Example From an Urban District in Central New Jersey" shows how typical comments were modified to be behaviorally specific and reflective of SEL skills. This district decided against using a rubric or Likert rating approach for the time being as it provided a feasible avenue to begin tracking these behaviors with hopes of further developing this system in the future.

o The "Example From an Urban Middle School in Central New Jersey" demonstrates a complete replacement of a comment section using a detailed rubric approach. This rubric approach addresses the absence or presence of a few very specific behaviors related to emotional control, one subskill related to self-management. This was done to make sure criteria and behaviors supporting ratings were as clear as possible for teachers, parents, and students without any other resources to understand what ratings meant.

o The "Example From a Middle School in Alaska" provides another rubric approach. This rubric differs in that a definition of the skill area is provided and each rubric rating level involves a broader menu of behaviors related to the overall skill category of social awareness.

o The "Example From the Kansas State Department of Education for K–2" demonstrates a Likert rating approach adopted statewide in recognition of the growing prominence of SEL and character-related skills in education at the state and federal level.

We envision a world where families, schools, and communities work together to promote students' success in school and life and to support the healthy development of all students. In this vision, students and adults are engaged life-long learners who are self-aware, caring and connected to others, and responsible in their decision making. Students and adults achieve to their fullest potential, and participate constructively in a democratic society.

— CASEL Vision, 2013

EXAMPLE FROM AN ELEMENTARY SCHOOL IN CENTRAL NEW JERSEY

In this elementary school, modifying report cards was done through the addition of a comment section labeled "Personal and Social Development." Administrators chose to maintain their current comment section and developed this list of eight comments based on the schoolwide Social Decision Making/Social Problem Solving Curriculum they had implemented.

"Is Able to Use 'Keep Calm'," for example, refers to student use of a relaxation exercise to assist a student in managing his or her level of stimulation or emotional arousal.

A three-point Likert scale format (i.e., check minus, check, check plus) is utilized for each comment to provide students and parents a detailed view of students' progress in social-emotional and character development skills known to be related to greater academic achievement.

Personal and Social Development Comments

1. Is able to follow classroom directions

2. Is able to follow rules

3. Is able to respect rights, feelings and property of others

4. Is able to identify and accept responsibility for actions

5. Is able to use B.E.S.T.* when addressing adults and peers

6. Is able to use "Keep Calm"

7. Is able to use Listening Position

8. Is able to use Speaker Power

*B.E.S.T. = Body Posture, Eye Contact, Say Nice or Appropriate Words, Tone of Voice

(Comments stem from Social Decision Making/Social Problem Solving Curriculum, www.researchpress.com)

Most people say that it is the intellect which makes a great scientist. They are wrong: it is character.

— Albert Einstein

EXAMPLE FROM AN URBAN DISTRICT IN CENTRAL NEW JERSEY

In this district, the comments being used on report cards were revised, replaced, or eliminated. This was done to enable teachers to comment on specific observable behaviors more closely related to the evidence-based SEL skills.

Each comment on this revised report card was given a rating on a five-point Likert scale, corresponding to the traditional A–F system of academic grading.

In the figure at the bottom of this page, an example of a simple revision of the comment "Is courteous and cooperative" is provided. Although this comment was clearly relevant to SEL, it addressed two different behaviors and, as a result, was not particularly clear in defining either. Separating a combined comment into two distinct skills allows each to be rated more accurately.

Revised Comment List From an Urban District

- Is considerate of others
- Works cooperatively
- Is respectful of other people's property
- Exercises self-control
- Completes work in a timely manner
- Shows responsibility for completing and returning homework
- Follows directions
- Uses time constructively
- Works independently
- Produces neat and legible work
- Shares willingly
- Takes responsibility for the care of classroom materials
- Takes turns and is attentive when others are speaking
- Accepts constructive suggestions/comments
- Demonstrates a positive attitude towards learning
- Shows confidence in self

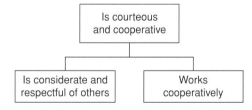

Education is not preparation for life; it is life itself.

— John Dewey

EXAMPLE FROM AN URBAN
MIDDLE SCHOOL IN CENTRAL NEW JERSEY

In this middle school, administrators and teachers actively collaborated and determined that a rubric approach would be most appropriate. Students in this format are rated utilizing the labels *emerging*, *developing*, *proficient*, and *distinguished*. The row labeled "General Description of Rankings" provides guiding criteria, including specific parameters around the amount of time and proficiency with which students should have demonstrated a skill to earn each specific rating. The row "Emotional Control" serves as an example of how a skill derived from the CASEL 5 can be broken down across the ratings in a clear, readily observable way.

The rubric categories are design to be positively framed. So a relatively low level of skill is referred to as *emerging*, an adequate level is seen as *developing*, and *proficiency* refers to the ability to use a skill across a wide range of appropriate situations and circumstances. Finally, *distinguished* skills signify not only possessing the skills across situations but also being able to instill those skills in others. An example can be found in Table 2.2.

Table 2.2 Scoring Rubric for Emotional Control

Scoring Criteria	N/A [0]	Emerging [1]	Developing [2]	Proficient [3]	Distinguished [4]
General Description of Rankings	No basis to judge.	Student is rarely able to perform this skill. (0–33% of the time)	Student's performance of this skill is not consistent. (34–66% of the time)	Student can consistently perform this skill. (67–90% of the time)	Demonstrates proficiency in all areas, with few errors. Student is able to apply skills in multiple situations and assisted others in learning skills. (90–100% of the time)
Emotional Control	No basis to judge.	Student is unable to recognize and/or regulate emotional state. This may result in frequent sadness, anxiety, and/or anger.	Student is able to recognize and regulate his/her own emotional state but not consistently. Student has a basic understanding of self-calming strategies.	Student is able to consistently recognize and regulate his/her own emotional state. Student can consistently use self-calming strategies.	Student is able to consistently recognize and regulate his/her own emotional state in many situations. Student can consistently use self-calming strategies even under great stress. Student coaches or teaches other students to recognize and regulate his or her emotional states.

EXAMPLE FROM A MIDDLE SCHOOL IN ALASKA

Social-emotional learning is widely implemented in this school district both through districtwide programming and a curriculum that infuses SEL concepts and skills into academic lessons. Students in this format are rated using the following labels: not yet within expectations, meets expectations, fully meets expectations, and exceeds expectations. A definition featuring the core competencies of self-awareness is provided in the column furthest to the left. Within each rating category, specific behaviors that compose these competencies are listed to assist teachers in making the most accurate ratings of SEL skills. Table 2.3 contains an example for social awareness.

Table 2.3 Scoring Rubric for Social Awareness

Scoring Criteria	Not Yet Within Expectations	Meets Expectations	Fully Meets Expectations	Exceeds Expectations
Social Awareness *Student Demonstrates:* • *Awareness of other people's emotions and perspectives* • *Consideration for others and a desire to positively contribute to his or her community* • *Awareness for cultural issues and a respect for human dignity and differences*	• Disrupts class discussions • Chooses not to get involved in helping others • Sometimes shows disrespect for peers; seems unaware of others' rights • Shows disrespect to adults (willful disobedience)	• Listens during class discussions • Helps friends • Often shows respect for peers • Often shows respect for adults, although may have trouble listening or following instructions occasionally	• Contributes to class discussions in a positive manner, listening to the perspective of others and sharing his/her own perspective • Helps others when appropriate (problem-solving bystander) • Shows respect for peers • Shows respect for adults and follows instructions and school rules	• Provides support and encouragement to his or her peers during class discussions • Is known as a positive leader amongst peers • Is fair and respectful; shows growing commitment to fair and just treatment for everyone

EXAMPLE FROM THE KANSAS STATE DEPARTMENT OF EDUCATION FOR K–2

In recognition of trends in research and policy recognizing the importance and impact of SEL and character in education, Kansas became one of the first states to develop a Likert rating approach for these skills at a state level (www.KSDE.org). A four-point Likert scale featuring *always, usually, rarely,* and *never* is utilized for all items listed on the following page, selected from a more comprehensive listing.

I. Social Awareness
1. Be aware of the thoughts, feelings, and perspectives of others.
2. Identify a range of emotions in others (for example, identify "sad" by facial expression; identify "mad" by tone of voice).
3. Identify possible causes for emotions (for example, losing dog may make you "sad"; your birthday may make you "happy").
4. Identify possible behaviors and anticipate reactions in response to a specific situation (for example, sharing candy may make your classmate smile; taking pencil may make your classmate yell at you).
5. Identify healthy personal hygiene habits.

II. Interpersonal Skills
1. Follow rules that respect classmates' needs and use polite language (for example, wait for his or her turn, stand in line, let classmate finish speaking).
2. Use "I" statements.
3. Pay attention to others when they are speaking.
4. Understand the importance of respecting personal space.
5. Recognize how facial expressions, body language, and tone communicate feelings.
6. Take turns and practice sharing.
7. Practice sharing encouraging comments.
8. Identify and demonstrate good manners.

STEPS TO EVALUATING CURRENT REPORT CARD COMMENTS IN YOUR SCHOOL

The following exercises have been developed to assist you in evaluating your own report cards on the extent to which SEL or character is currently represented by comments, degree of comment clarity and specificity, and relevance of comments to the most prevalent behaviors in your district. The exercises can be used in combination or in isolation to guide your thinking as you determine which behaviors are most essential for your school or district.

Table 2.4 Steps to Evaluating Current Report Card Comments in Your School

EXERCISE #1

Using the CASEL definitions and/or character definitions provided, examine the report card comments currently in use in your school. When comments seem to fit into the CASEL 5 or 7 Character Strengths (see Table 1.1), list them within the category represented. When comments do not fit, write them down on a separate list. After all are listed, see what general categories these comments may represent, and list them.

GOAL: Determine the extent to which SEL and character are represented by current report card comments.

GUIDING QUESTIONS: Which domains are represented? Which still need to be addressed?

EXERCISE #2

Rank current comments based on their clarity and specificity. Those that receive the highest ranking should be easily interpretable and clear across teachers, parents, and students. Those with the lowest ranking should be ambiguous, unclear, or refer to multiple behaviors or skills within the same comment. Remember, the goal of comments is to provide feedback on specific behaviors so that teachers, parents, and students can be aligned in interpreting, understanding, and promoting behaviors that best support learning and achievement.

GOAL: Identify the extent to which comments currently in use are providing clear feedback on specific behaviors.

GUIDING QUESTIONS: Which comments are most effective in providing specific feedback? Do these comments address the most essential student behaviors? (Consider both experiences in your school as is emphasized in Exercise #3 and the research supporting SEL and character.) Which comments are the least specific and, thus, most likely to need revision?

EXERCISE #3

Rank comments currently being utilized in your school by perceived relevance to the behaviors students demonstrate most often. (Table 3.2, titled "Common Characteristics of Student Behavior and the Overlap With SEL," may be helpful.)

GOAL: Identify to what extent comments provide an opportunity to communicate on the behaviors that occur most often in your school.

GUIDING QUESTIONS: Are the behaviors that occur most often represented? If not, would it be appropriate to include these behaviors in a future comment system? If you also completed Exercise #1, which of the comments relevant to SEL or character are ranked highest and lowest? How would SEL or character domains and skills not represented rank in terms of relevance to student behaviors?

3

ADAPTING YOUR REPORT CARD COMMENTS FOR SEL AND/OR CHARACTER

Utility: After seeing a glimpse of how this is a flexible process influenced by many factors (e.g., existing programming) and examining some of those factors through reflection exercises (i.e., at the end of Chapter 2), it is time to think more critically about the match between those factors and some recommended options for your school or district. This chapter is designed to provide guidance in linking key considerations of current programming with conceptual and practical advantages of rating SEL, character, or both, as well as advantages and disadvantages of Likert versus rubric rating approaches.

Maximizing Guide Resources: Sections of this chapter may be useful to distribute to any key decision makers, including administrators and staff heavily involved in the process (e.g., school or district leadership teams), either before or as part of an in-meeting exercise to promote appropriate consideration and discussion of which approaches fit best for your school or district.

Key Takeaway and Reflection Points:

- Deciding to emphasize SEL, character, or both may be influenced by school culture, goals, values, curriculum, and more.

- Existing programming may heavily guide what behaviors to emphasize and have implications for the implementation process. Does your school's current programming emphasize behaviors related to SEL, character, or both?

- Which practical and conceptual advantages discussed are most essential or important for your school?

- Would teachers, students, and parents respond better and be more interested in more stable character virtues or more behaviorally specific SEL skills? Consider how this decision will impact which style of rating may be more appropriate.

- Is a cohesive combination of character and SEL already present in your school? If not, would such a combination be possible and in line with school culture? Which style of rating would best support such a combination for teachers, students, and staff?

IN THIS CHAPTER

It is likely that you are not simply interested in making your current comment system more clear but also including elements of SEL and/or character into an existing behavior rating format or a rating format created in this process. Doing so recognizes the research showing that students' SEL and character virtues are empirical indicators of success in academics and future life. More to the point, deficiencies noted likely also contribute to academic and behavior or disciplinary shortcomings, and having a systematic way to monitor and identify progress in these areas over time for all students can prompt strategic early intervention. Therefore, this chapter provides specific guidance in determining whether to emphasize SEL, character, or both and how to choose a rating system best aligned with school and district goals and practices.

GUIDING QUESTIONS IN DECIDING TO EMPHASIZE SEL, CHARACTER, OR BOTH

- What are the goals of your school or district?
- How would the culture of the surrounding community influence an emphasis on character or SEL? What is the current climate of the school or district?
- Are there schoolwide or districtwide programs currently in place? Do they address and/or incorporate character or SEL?
- Does the curriculum of your school create natural or potential opportunities for an emphasis on SEL or character?
- How might the developmental and grade level(s) of the students in your school impact their ability to develop competence in either area? (See Tables 3.2 and 3.3 and the online supplement "SEL Skill Trajectory, Grades 1–12" available at http://resource .corwin.com/EliasReportCard.)

ARRIVING AT A DECISION ON AN APPROACH TO INTEGRATING SEL AND/OR CHARACTER INTO REPORT CARDS

Schools arrive at a decision to integrate SEL and/or character into their report cards in one of two ways, generally:

- Option 1: Schools have made a commitment to build students' social-emotional competencies and/or character and now wish to have a formal, explicit, systematic way of assessing progress.
- Option 2: Schools realize the importance of SEL and/or character for their broader purposes of developing the whole student, fostering academic achievement, promoting positive behavior, and creating a positive culture and climate for learning. In these circumstances, schools realize that it is essential to

highlight SEL and/or character on the report card to provide focus on these areas for teachers, students, administrators, and parents.

Option 1: Aligning SEL and/or Character Report Card Assessment With Existing Programming

The task under Option 1 is inductive. A school must systematically examine what it is currently doing related to SEL and/or character and then determine what is most important to assess. (The Association for Supervision and Curriculum Development's [ASCD] *Promoting Social and Emotional Learning: Guidelines for Educators* provides a comprehensive guide to carrying out such an assessment [Elias et al., 1997].) The task of self-examination and prioritization has many benefits for a school as it increases the chances of aligning existing program elements toward the goal of greater synergy of impact. This includes delineating the elements that are common across different efforts so that there can be a more explicit focus on them. Tasks in the service of greater synergy are essential for optimizing student impact. Note that this task can also uncover gaps or inconsistencies in programming. It may be the case that when initial assessment priorities are determined, there is a clear understanding in the school that the overall programming for SEL and/or character is going to be revisited with an eye toward the goal of creating more continuity, consistency, and coordination. Hence, the initial report card modifications should be viewed as interim, with revisions expected within perhaps two to three years.

Comprehensive Guide ←

Option 2: Determining SEL and/or Character Priorities for Report Card Assessment and Creating Relevant Programming

The task under Option 2 is deductive. The school comes together for a conversation to identify focal SEL skills and/or values it wishes to emphasize. The conversations allow educators and other staff to share observations about what it is that students need to succeed in school and life, in college and careers, based on their experiences and the literature. In this sense, the school is establishing its own unique identity, a sense of what the school would like to impart to students who pass through its doors over multiple years. Once areas have been identified, subgroups of staff help to pare them down so they are developmentally appropriate to the school's population and can be operationalized using the procedures presented in this Guide. The subsequent part of this task, however, is developing programming that will build these prioritized skills and values systematically and comprehensively across grade levels. That is, what is important is not only worth measuring but also worth building up. One might even say that the latter is less a programming option than a moral imperative. Resources exist to guide the development of such programming (e.g., Beland, 2003; CASEL, 2003; Durlak, Domitrovich, Weissberg, & Gullotta, 2015; Elias & Arnold, 2006; Nucci, Narvaez, & Krettenauer, 2014).

THEORETICAL AND PRACTICAL CONSIDERATIONS OF EMPHASIZING SEL, CHARACTER, OR BOTH

In addition to current school programming, it is important for educators to consider the current manner in which SEL skills and character development are being defined, researched, and applied. While conceptually, many SEL skills and aspects of character development have clear areas of overlap, there are also obvious differences that have driven each area's respective efforts in research and application. Potential reasons for choosing to emphasize SEL or character are summarized in the Table 3.1 on page 26.

Perhaps the most fundamental difference is that current evidence-based SEL skill categories have been consistently rooted in specific, observable behaviors to the greatest extent possible. As a result, each of the CASEL 5 skill categories contains subcategories made up of a menu of observable behaviors grouped together to show how these specific behaviors cumulatively represent skill development and acquisition. This approach has enabled developmentally sensitive SEL skill trajectories to emerge and be implemented in state standards such as Illinois, where specific skill-based behaviors are broken down by grade level, from elementary to high school. To add further developmental consideration, a list of common student behaviors seen across grade levels conceptually mapped onto CASEL 5 is provided in Table 3.2.

Character

Being that character virtues are not as well suited for developmental mapping of clear, observable behaviors but still have obvious and well-supported evidence to be promoted and assessed, this Guide follows the approach taken by leaders in the field of character education and psychology (e.g., Duckworth, Peterson, and Seligman). Character virtues are framed by experts as indicators with greater stability over time, and thus, the need for a clear developmental trajectory of trait development is not as heavily prioritized. This means that indicators of character virtues will remain relatively constant across grade levels and that raters can use similar subcategories composed of broader behavioral groupings to measure virtue development. In order to add further developmental consideration, this Guide provides a table of common student behaviors seen across grade levels conceptually mapped onto the seven character virtues proposed (see Table 3.3, "Common Characteristics of Student Behaviors by Grade and the Overlap With Character Virtues").

How Character and SEL Differ

Character development is certainly connected to behavioral indicators and, thus, shares some of the benefits listed above. However, the breakdown of each trait into specific observable behaviors mapped onto a clear developmental trajectory appears to have yet to occur with consistency, if at all. Some barriers to this process are similar to those encountered initially in SEL and may include the diverse array of attributes considered to be representative of some dimension of character and the selective inclusion of certain character traits in an array of theories of student development. However, clear conceptual barriers emerge even in simply reviewing particular character virtues included in this Guide. Consider, for example, how one would develop developmentally appropriate specific behavioral indicators for a trait such as zest (i.e., approaching life with excitement and energy and feeling alive and activated). There are many variables that may mediate how zest manifests, such as one's underlying personality structure and culture. Determining the degree of enthusiasm an individual should outwardly display at various developmental levels is a tricky and, in some contexts, sensitive task. While most would likely agree that approaching life with enthusiasm is beneficial, few are likely to feel confident in designating what an appropriate level of enthusiasm might be for a particular grade level, let alone how that would be assessed. Some of these difficulties and issues of sensitivity are also inherent in some SEL skill categories. However, the broad menu of observable SEL skills allows raters to select indicators to promote attunement with the population being assessed.

Combining SEL and Character

SEL skills and character traits can be handpicked and combined by districts and schools to create a custom rating system that entails the most attractive and fitting aspects of each. States such as Kansas have now developed standards that combine both SEL and character, which is typically referred to as social, emotional, and character development (SECD). While there are many intuitive advantages of integrating the two, assessments supported in research that encompass aspects of both SEL and character development are not readily identifiable as this is an area that has not been as widely reviewed or investigated. This is likely due to the multifaceted nature and numerous difficulties encountered in developing measures to assess even individual SEL skill or character virtue development, let alone each respective skill or virtue grouping comprehensively, or the even more complex task of integrating the assessment of both SEL and character into a single measure. This may result in challenges for schools in attempting to find model methods of assessment to emulate in adapting report card comment sections. As methods of assessment specifically intended for either SEL or character are developed and better established in research, it is likely that measures of SECD will emerge. If other states decide to implement standards of SECD, this body of research is likely to emerge more rapidly. Although the current state of research may not reflect it, the assessment of SEL and character on a single instrument, such as "the other side of the report card," is likely to emerge in the future. Schools willing to implement programming consistent with SECD and develop innovative approaches to assessing SECD may serve to advance the research and the practice of integrating these two valuable areas of student development. Table 3.1 provides a summary of considerations regarding the relative advantages of an emphasis on SEL or character.

Table 3.1 Overview of Potential Advantages of Emphasizing SEL or Character

CASEL 5 SEL Skills	Character Virtues
• Self-awareness • Self-management • Social awareness • Relationship skills • Responsible decision making	• Zest • Grit • Self-control • Optimism • Gratitude • Social intelligence • Curiosity
Potential Advantages of SEL	**Potential Advantages of Character**
• Broader menu of specific behaviors to choose from when selecting what to assess • Greater sensitivity to specific behavioral skill development over time • Stronger likelihood for inter-rater reliability as rating items are more commonly defined as specific, observable behaviors • Ability to orient new teachers or teachers working with a new grade level regarding what to expect in terms of the behavioral manifestation of various skills for students at that developmental level • Connection to specific behavior relevant to academic achievement is clear	• Indicators are fewer but are applicable across a larger grade range, indicating less need for developmentally driven adaptation. • Most character virtues are commonly understood—"you know it when you see it." • The greater applicability of fewer items yields a stronger likelihood of tracking progress on any item that remains constant over a longer period of time. • Staff and community members' conceptualizations of indicators of character virtues typically emerge in common discussions of character and personality. • Districts and schools are able to autonomously generate more specific skill indicators and other methods to promote reliability across raters, customized to local norms and the respective student population as needed.

Table 3.2 Common Characteristics of Student Behavior and the Overlap With SEL

	Self-Awareness & Self-Management	Social Awareness & Relationship Skills	Responsible Decision Making
Grade 1	• Enthusiastic, energetic, noisy, and active • Thrive on encouragement • Can tire easily • Take on projects that are too big for them • Engage in more elaborate and dramatic play • Enjoy explaining their thoughts (e.g., how something happened or how things work) • Dislike taking risks and making mistakes	• Competitive • Start seeking first best friend • Thrive on encouragement • Sensitive to criticism (big or small) • Can be bossy • Ask many questions • Like to work alone or with a friend • Enjoy one-on-one conversations	• Begin to test the limits of authority • Begin to conceptualize cause and effect

Table 3.2 (Continued)

	Self-Awareness & Self-Management	Social Awareness & Relationship Skills	Responsible Decision Making
Grade 2	• Are self-focused • Have distinct likes and dislikes • Can be moody • Struggle to focus on things that are physically far away (e.g., the board) • Struggle under time pressure	• Can be shy • Need security and structure • Often find group work overwhelming • May change friends quickly • Need frequent "check-ins" with a teacher • Show significant growth in listening skills	• Increasingly interested in logic, classification, and how things work
Grade 3	• Adjust well to change • Willing to take risks • Take on more than they can handle • Have a limited attention span but can become engrossed in an activity	• Enjoy socializing and working in groups • Eager for approval from adults and peers • Tend to exaggerate • Tend to listen well but have so many ideas that they may not remember what they heard	• Concerned with fairness and justice • Often hurrying
Grade 4	• Criticize selves and complain a lot (i.e., often say, "I hate it," "I can't," or "It's boring") • Need adult lightheartedness, humor, and encouragement to lighten their moods • Work hard and pay attention to detail but may jump between interests	• Like to work with the same gender • Can work in groups but with lots of arguing • Worry about world events, parents' health, friends, and school	• Begin to see the bigger world, including issues of justice and fairness
Grade 5	• Quick to anger and quick to forgive • Hardworking and take pride in schoolwork	• Eager to reach out to others (e.g., team sports, clubs, community service, etc.) • Competitive but also cooperative • Listen well but also enjoy talking and explaining	• Open to learning mediation and problem-solving skills
Grade 6	• Moody • Self-absorbed • Need adult empathy, humor, and light attitude to help them take things less seriously	• Easily embarrassed and need to "save face" in front of peers • Need lots of time to talk with peers • Worry about peer-group belonging • Beginning of peak time for harassment, bullying, and intimidation, often to secure peer position and as response to insecurity (through Grade 7)	• Like to challenge rules, argue, and test limits

(Continued)

Table 3.2 (Continued)

	Self-Awareness & Self-Management	Social Awareness & Relationship Skills	Responsible Decision Making
Grade 7	• Capable of insight • Can take on major responsibilities such as running a school store or raising money • Careless with "unimportant things," such as cleaning their rooms and keeping track of assignments • Can set goals and concentrate well	• Peer opinions matter more than those of teachers and parents • More willing to accept guidance from adults other than teachers or parents • Capable of empathy • Understand and enjoy sarcasm, double meanings, and more sophisticated jokes	• Very interested in civics, history, current events, environmental issues, and social justice
Grade 8	• Moody and sensitive • Anger can flare up suddenly • Very concerned about personal appearance • Spend hours on the phone or computer and with video games and TV • Tentative, worried, and unwilling to take risks on tough intellectual tasks	• Prefer working alone • A lot of pressure in what to wear, how to talk, etc. • Answer parents with a single word or loud, extreme language • Better at written work than oral expression • Starting to enjoy thinking about many sides of an issue	• Challenge the ideas and authority of parents and teachers • Interested in fairness, justice, and discrimination
Grade 9	• Need adult connection even while fighting for their own identities • Need adults to listen and negotiate rules and requirements • Can be extremely oppositional • Typically loud and rambunctious	• Fiercely criticize parents • Can rise up to leadership challenges in student council, peer tutoring, etc. • Work well in small groups • Better at thinking abstractly	• Can be influenced by peer pressure or perceived peer perception in decision making
Grades 10–12	• Growing consideration about career and college goals, sometimes unrealistically or not connected to current behaviors	• Close friendships more important • Want to have confidantes among peers and adults, though not necessarily parents	• Decision-making patterns become more consistent regarding risk, consideration of multiple options, and long- and short-term consequences • Improved ability to bounce back from setbacks

Table 3.3 Common Characteristics of Student Behavior by Grade and the Overlap with Character Virtues

	Zest	Self-Control	Gratitude	Curiosity	Optimism	Grit	Social Intelligence
Grade 1	• Enthusiastic and energetic • Thrive on encouragement • Engaged in more elaborate and dramatic play	• Enjoy explaining their thoughts (e.g., how something happened or how things work) • Sensitive to criticism		• Ask many questions • Enjoy one-on-one conversation • Begin to conceptualize cause and effect • Begin to test the limits of authority	• Sensitive to criticism	• Can tire easily • Take on projects that are too big for them • Dislike taking risks and making mistakes	• Competitive • Start seeking first best friend • Can be bossy • Like to work alone or with a friend
Grade 2	• Have distinct likes and dislikes	• Can be moody • Struggle to focus on things that are physically far away (e.g., the board)		• Increasingly interested in logic, classification, and how things work • Show significant growth in listening skills	• Need frequent check-ins with teacher	• Struggle under time pressure • Are self-focused	• Can be shy • Need security and structure • Often find group work overwhelming • May change friends quickly
Grade 3	• Tend to exaggerate	• Eager for approval from adults and peers • Often hurrying		• Concerned with fairness and justice	• Adjust well to change	• Willing to take risks • Take on more than they can handle • Have a limited attention span but can become engrossed in an activity	• Enjoy socializing and working in groups • Tend to listen well but have so many ideas that they may not remember what they heard

(Continued)

Table 3.3 (Continued)

	Zest	Self-Control	Gratitude	Curiosity	Optimism	Grit	Social Intelligence
Grade 4	• Like to work with the same gender • May jump between interests • Love language and word play	• Need adult lightheartedness, humor, and encouragement to lighten their moods • Work hard and pay attention to detail • May jump between interests • Criticize selves	• Need adults to be patient	• Begin to see the bigger world, including issues of justice and fairness • Need adults to explain things clearly • Want factual explanations and enjoy scientific exploration	• Worry about world events, parents' health, friends, and school	• Complain a lot (i.e., often say, "I hate it," "I can't," or "It's boring")	• Can work in groups but with lots of arguing • May form cliques
Grade 5	• Enjoy adult recognition	• Quick to anger and quick to forgive • Need adult empathy, humor, and light attitude to help them take things less seriously	• Eager to reach out to others (e.g., community service or tutoring)	• Listen well but also enjoy talking and explaining • Enjoy collecting, organizing, and classifying • Like rules and logic	• Quick to anger and quick to forgive	• Hardworking and take pride in schoolwork	• More interested in groups (e.g., team sports and clubs) • Competitive but also cooperative • Open to learning mediation and problem-solving skills
Grade 6	• Would rather learn new skills than review or improve previous work • Enjoy adult tasks, though may outwardly fuss while secretly enjoying the work	• Moody • Need adult empathy, humor, and light attitude to help them take things less seriously	• Self-absorbed	• Like to challenge rules, argue, and test limits • Can think abstractly • Beginning to challenge adult explanations and own assumptions	• Enjoy using their developing thinking skills to do brain teasers and puzzles		• Easily embarrassed and need to "save face" in front of peers • Need lots of time to talk with peers • Worry about peer-group belonging

Grade 7	• Very energetic but need lots of sleep, exercise, and food • May begin to excel at a subject or skill • Enthusiastic about schoolwork seen as purposeful (e.g., science experiments or drama productions)	• Capable of insight • Can set goals and concentrate well	• More willing to accept guidance from adults other than teachers and parents	• Very interested in civics, history, current events, environmental issues, and social justice • Question and argue with adults about rules	• Need adults to listen to ideas	• Can take on major responsibilities such as running a school store or raising money • Careless with "unimportant things," such as cleaning their rooms and keeping track of assignments	• Peer opinions matter more than those of teachers and parents • Capable of empathy • Understand and enjoy sarcasm, double meanings, more sophisticated jokes
Grade 8	• Spend hours on the phone or computer and with video games and TV • Very energetic but need lots of sleep, exercise, and food	• Moody and sensitive • Anger can flare up suddenly • Answer parents with single word or loud, extreme language	• Like to be left alone when home	• Starting to enjoy thinking about many sides of an issue • Challenge the ideas and authority of parents and teachers • Interested in fairness, justice, and discrimination	• Tentative, worried, and unwilling to take risks on tough intellectual tasks	• Prefer working alone • Need short, predictable assignments to build good habits	• Very concerned about personal appearance • A lot of pressure in what to wear, how to talk, etc. • Better at written work than oral expression • Can easily hurt others' feelings
Grade 9	• Typically loud and rambunctious • Very energetic but need lots of sleep, exercise, and food • Enjoy individual skills (music, art, etc.)	• Mimic adult behavior but resent adult lectures	• Need adults to listen and negotiate rules and requirements • Need adult connection even while fighting for their own identities • Fiercely criticize parents	• Can be extremely oppositional • Better at thinking abstractly • Like technology and learning how things work	• Respond well to variety and challenge	• Can rise up to leadership challenges in student council, peer tutoring, etc. • Often say, "I'm bored," to mean, "I don't understand"	• Work well in small groups • Work hard at creating teen subculture

CONSIDERATIONS IN DECIDING BETWEEN LIKERT AND RUBRIC RATING APPROACHES

Likert Rating Approach

The Likert approach involves the use of specific anchor points with minimal description. Descriptions typically involve the use of general terms (e.g., never, sometimes, often, or always) but can also be more specific (e.g., 0–33%, 34–66%, 67–90%, 91–100%).

ADVANTAGES

- Requires minimal space
- Anchors can be based in extent of skill development, frequency of skill demonstration, and consistency of skill display, enabling schools to determine how to best rate skills in their environment

DISADVANTAGES

- Lack of detailed descriptors enhances potential for different interpretations of skills across raters, possibly decreasing reliability

Rubric Rating Approach

Rubrics utilize sentences or paragraphs to describe each potential rating in detail. Specific anchors may also be used; however, the emphasis is placed on the detailed description of the behaviors being rated at each of the possible levels.

ADVANTAGES

- The detail of descriptions may also enhance consistency and reliability across raters.
- In-depth description provides firm guidance for raters to reference in decision making.

DISADVANTAGES

- Detailed descriptions require additional space on the physical report card or other accommodations for carrying out the ratings.

Anchor Points

Anchor points can be determined based on the range of the Likert scale used. They can also be used as additional descriptors in rubric approaches that are specific in the behaviors rated. Generally, anchors should be relatively evenly distributed across the Likert categories. A four-point Likert scale, for example, might involve the lowest rating (e.g., 1) indicating a behavior is displayed less than 25% of the time, a rating of 2 indicating 26 to 50% of the time, a 3 indicating 51 to 75% of the time, and a 4 indicating 75 to 100% of the time. However, it can be valuable to distribute anchor points differently to create greater sensitivity to a particular threshold of skill development and demonstration. In the example ranges provided in Table 3.6 on page 35, for instance, anchor points are distributed more broadly among lower ratings so as to reserve the highest rating (e.g., a 4, indicating demonstration 91 to 100% of the time).

This creates a more selective threshold for identifying those students who very consistently demonstrate the skill and help others to learn it. Perhaps in your school or district, it is helpful to identify the most proficient students with greater sensitivity for various purposes, such as being better able to track outcomes for that group or pair students based on strengths and area in need of improvement.

Recommendations

Reviewing the examples below may be beneficial in envisioning how each of these approaches might take form. The Likert format may be most appropriate when a very clear understanding of what is being rated is communicated. This can be accomplished through the specificity of the item (e.g., the description of a clear and observable behavior), description of key example behaviors that support the rating (e.g., provided concisely in list form under each item or as a rating aid in supplemental materials on the school's website), or a strong definition of the skill or virtue (e.g., as part of a quick reference guide to ratings). An example of the kind of supplemental material that a district may choose to place online is a developmentally adapted SEL Likert rating system progression by grade level.

Rubric formats may be most appropriate in contexts where space is not a strong limiting factor (e.g., online). Also, rubrics are helpful when complex definitions are necessary to accurately define a combination of behaviors or concepts are difficult to break down into single observable behaviors. Likert and rubric components should be considered flexibly. It may be helpful to conceptualize these two approaches as existing on a continuum as there are likely many combinations of components related to these two rating styles.

Additional Considerations for Comparing Likert Versus Rubric Rating Approaches

- Which style of rating do teachers favor in your district? Which rating approach is more aligned with the type of feedback staff would like to provide?
- Which form of feedback is more likely to be meaningful to parents and students? What is the level of familiarity with SEL and character? Is the depth provided by the rubric necessary?
- Which approach would you place more confidence in if a potential use of ratings is to view trends on the individual, school, and district level? Is either more feasible for this purpose in your school or district?
- Could supplemental materials be used to strengthen either approach if supplied to staff, parents, or others (e.g., use of materials in this Guide, such as Table 3.3, "Common Characteristics of Student Behavior by Grade and the Overlap With Character Virtues," and the online supplement "SEL Skill Trajectory, Grades 1–12" available at http://resource.corwin.com/EliasReportCard)?

- How can you determine if the approach you chose is sound? (See Chapter 7, "Checklist of Important Considerations," to help evaluate your adapted comment section.)

Table 3.4 Example: SEL Likert Rating System

SEL Likert Ratings by Marking Period	MP 1	MP 2	MP 3	MP 4
Recognizes and regulates emotions using self-calming strategies				
Exhibits self-worth and self-confidence by engaging in positive self-talk				
Demonstrates impulse control				
Recognizes and respects the feelings and perspectives of others				
Recognizes and utilizes school, family, and/or community resources to support academic, social, and/or emotional functioning				
Establishes and maintains cooperative relationships				
Constructively resolves interpersonal conflict to best meet the needs of all parties involved				
Considers and evaluates consequences to decisions				
Engages in group decision making productively by discussing and considering the perspectives and opinions of groupmates				

Each skill is rated on a scale from 0 to 4, where 0 = strongly disagree, 1 = disagree, 2 = neither agree nor disagree, 3 = agree, 4 = strongly agree (i.e., 4 is the best score).

Table 3.5 Example: Character Likert Rating System

Character Likert Ratings by Marking Period	MP 1	MP 2	MP 3	MP 4
Shows enthusiasm				
Tries very hard even after experiencing failure				
Pays attention and resists distractions				
Remains calm even when criticized or otherwise provoked				
Gets over frustrations and setbacks quickly				
Recognizes and shows opportunities for others				
Is able to find solutions during conflicts with others				
Asks and answers questions to deepen understanding				
Engages in group decision making productively by discussing and considering the perspectives and opinions of groupmates				

Each character-based skill is rated on a scale from 1 to 5, where 1 = very much unlike the student, 2 = unlike the student, 3 = somewhat like the student, 4 = like the student, 5 = very much like the student (i.e., 5 is the best score).

Table 3.6 Example: SEL Rubric Rating System

Scoring Criteria	Not Applicable (N/A) [0]	Emerging (EM) [1]	Developing (DE) [2]	Proficient (PR) [3]	Distinguished (D) [4]
General Description of Rankings	No basis to judge. (Select if have not witnessed these behaviors and attributes at all)	Student is rarely able to perform this skill. (0–33% of the time)	Student's performance of this skill is not consistent. (34–66% of the time)	Student can consistently perform this skill. (67–90% of the time)	Demonstrates proficiency in all areas with few, if any, errors. Student is able to apply skills in multiple situations. Student assisted others in learning skills. (91–100% of the time)
SELF-AWARENESS AND SELF-MANAGEMENT					
Emotional Control	No basis to judge.	Student is unable to recognize and/or regulate his or her own emotional state. This may result in frequent sadness, anxiety, and/or anger.	Student is able to recognize and regulate his or her own emotional state but not consistently. Student has a basic understanding of self-calming strategies.	Student is able to consistently recognize and regulate his or her own emotional state. Student can consistently use self-calming strategies.	Student is able to consistently recognize and regulate his or her own emotional state in many situations. Student can consistently use self-calming strategies even under great stress. Student coaches or teaches other students to recognize and regulate their emotional states.
Self-Worth and Self-Confidence	No basis to judge.	Student has low self-worth and low self-confidence.	Student's self-worth and confidence may fluctuate a lot across situations and/or time. Student has a basic understanding of positive self-talk.	Student's self-worth and self-confidence are often positive. Student can consistently use positive self-talk.	Student's self-worth and self-confidence are consistently strong, without being arrogant or narcissistic. Student can consistently use positive self-talk, even under great stress. Student coaches or teaches other students to feel positive about themselves.
Impulse Control	No basis to judge.	Student appears to be unable to control his or her impulses. Student needs chronic assistance to stay on task.	Student acts impulsively but can often rein it in with outside assistance. Outside assistance may be needed occasionally.	Student is able to maintain self-control over a range of situations. Outside assistance is not usually needed.	Student is able to maintain self-control over a range of situations, even when it is tempting to give in to immediate gratification. Outside assistance is very rarely needed. Student coaches or teaches other students how to maintain self-control and their impulses.

(Continued)

Table 3.6 (Continued)

SOCIAL AWARENESS AND RELATIONSHIP SKILLS

Scoring Criteria	Not Applicable (N/A) [0]	Emerging (EM) [1] (0–33% of the time)	Developing (DE) [2] (34–66% of the time)	Proficient (PR) [3] (67–90% of the time)	Distinguished (D) [4] (91–100% of the time)
Recognize and Respect the Feelings and Perspectives of Others	No basis to judge.	Student is unable to recognize and/or respond appropriately to the emotional state or perspective of others. This results in a lack of empathy and minimal consideration of others when acting.	Student's ability to recognize and/or respond to the emotional state or perspective of others may fluctuate a lot across situations. The student has some skills in recognizing common emotions (e.g., mad, sad, or happy) and demonstrates consideration of others when acting sometimes (e.g., provides support to peers in need).	Student can consistently recognize and respond to the emotional states or perspectives of others. The student demonstrates awareness and consideration of others when acting sometimes (e.g., provides support to peers in need) and can actively engage in perspective-taking.	Student can consistently recognize and respond to the emotional states or perspectives of others. The student demonstrates awareness and consideration of others when acting. Student coaches or teaches peers to recognize others' emotions and to engage in perspective-taking to promote empathy.
Resource Recognition and Use	No basis to judge.	Student is unable to recognize family, school, and community resources for academic and/or personal support. Student does not readily seek help.	Student is aware of some family, school, and community resources for academic and/or personal support. Student seeks help when needed but inconsistently or only when instructed to do so by an adult.	Student is aware of many family, school, and community resources for academic and/or personal support. Student consistently seeks help when needed with little or no instruction from an adult.	Student is aware of many family, school, and community resources for academic and/or personal support. Student readily and consistently seeks help when needed. Student coaches or teaches peers about various resources and encourages them to seek help when needed.
Establishing and Maintaining Cooperative Relationships	No basis to judge.	Student is unable to use communication and social skills to interact effectively with others.	Student demonstrates some communication and social skills but inconsistently interacts effectively with others. Student is able to establish few relationships and/or has difficulty maintaining cooperative relationships.	Student consistently utilizes communication and social skills to interact effectively with others. Student is able to establish and maintain multiple cooperative relationships.	Student consistently utilizes communication and social skills to interact effectively with others. Student is able to establish and maintain multiple cooperative relationships. Student teaches peers to utilize communication and social skills to engage in cooperative relationships.

Scoring Criteria	Not Applicable (N/A) [0]	Emerging (EM) [1] (0–33% of the time)	Developing (DE) [2] (34–66% of the time)	Proficient (PR) [3] (67–90% of the time)	Distinguished (D) [4] (91–100% of the time)
Resolving Interpersonal Conflict	No basis to judge.	Student is unable to distinguish between constructive and destructive ways of dealing with conflict or to identify positive supports to go to in conflict situations.	Student is able to distinguish between constructive and destructive ways of dealing with conflict but inconsistently employs a constructive approach. Student struggles to identify how all parties might get their needs met in a fair manner and to identify positive supports to go to in conflict situations.	Student consistently employs a constructive approach to resolving conflict in which he or she attempts to meet the needs of all parties in a fair manner. Student readily identifies and accesses positive social supports to go to in conflict situations.	Student consistently employs a constructive approach to resolving conflict in which he or she attempts to meet the needs of all parties in a fair manner. Student readily identifies and accesses positive social supports to go to in conflict situations. Student teaches or coaches others how to constructively resolve conflict.

RESPONSIBLE DECISION-MAKING

Scoring Criteria	Not Applicable (N/A) [0]	Emerging (EM) [1] (0–33% of the time)	Developing (DE) [2] (34–66% of the time)	Proficient (PR) [3] (67–90% of the time)	Distinguished (D) [4] (91–100% of the time)
Independent Decision Making	No basis to judge.	Student is unable to consider consequences of decisions fully, including issues of ethics, safety, social norms, and respect.	Student inconsistently considers and evaluates consequences of decisions, including issues of ethics, safety, social norms, and respect, in order to make decisions that contribute to the well-being of him or herself and/or others.	Student consistently evaluates consequences of decisions, including issues of ethics, safety, social norms, and respect, in order to make decisions that contribute to the well-being of him or herself, others, the school, and the community.	Student consistently evaluates consequences of decisions, including issues of ethics, safety, social norms, and respect, in order to make decisions that contribute to the well-being of him or herself, others, the school, and the community. Student coaches or teaches peers to make responsible decisions.
Group Decision Making	No basis to judge.	Student is unable to participate in productive discussion with others to reach a decision.	Student inconsistently participates productively in discussions with others to evaluate consequences and reach a group decision. Student inconsistently considers the perspectives and interests of groupmates in the decision-making process.	Student consistently participates productively in discussions with others by considering and responding to the perspectives and interests of groupmates while evaluating consequences and reaching a group decision.	Student consistently participates productively in discussions with others by considering and responding to the perspectives and interests of groupmates while evaluating consequences and reaching a group decision. Student coaches or teaches peers to engage productively in the group decision-making process.

Table 3.7 Example: Character Rubric Rating System

Scoring Criteria	Not Applicable (N/A) [0]	Absent (A) [1]	Basic (B) [2]	Contributor (C) [3]	Leader (L) [4]
General Description of Rankings	No basis to judge. (Select if you have not witnessed these behaviors and attributes at all).	Student is rarely able to demonstrate attribute indicators. (0–33% of the time)	Student's demonstration of attribute indicators is not consistent. (34–66% of the time)	Student can consistently demonstrate attribute indicators. (67–90% of the time)	Demonstrates all attribute indicators with few, if any, inconsistencies. Student is able to apply attribute indicators in multiple situations. Student assisted others in learning the attribute. (91–100% of the time)
Zest	No basis to judge.	Student does not participate or demonstrate enthusiasm toward most tasks.	Student participates occasionally and inconsistently demonstrates enthusiasm toward tasks.	Student consistently participates and approaches many tasks with enthusiasm.	Student consistently participates and approaches most tasks with enthusiasm. Student's enthusiasm and energy invigorates others.
Self-Control	No basis to judge.	Student is unable to recognize and/or regulate his or her own emotional state or impulses. Student needs chronic assistance to remain calm and stay on task.	Student is able to recognize and regulate his or her own emotional state and impulses but inconsistently. Student has a basic understanding of strategies to remain on task and calm.	Student is able to consistently recognize and regulate his or her emotional state and impulses. Student remains calm and on task, at times, even when criticized or otherwise provoked.	Student is able to consistently recognize and regulate his or her emotional state and impulses. Student remains calm and on task even when criticized or otherwise provoked. Student coaches or teaches other students how to maintain self-control over emotions and impulses.
Gratitude	No basis to judge.	Student is unable to recognize or show appreciation for others and his or her opportunities.	Student inconsistently recognizes and shows appreciation for others and his or her opportunities.	Student consistently recognizes and shows appreciation for others and his or her opportunities.	Student consistently recognizes and shows appreciation for others and his or her opportunities. Student coaches or teaches other students how to experience and demonstrate gratitude.

Scoring Criteria	Not Applicable (N/A) [0]	Absent (A) [1]	Basic (B) [2]	Contributor (C) [3]	Leader (L) [4]
Curiosity	No basis to judge.	Student does not demonstrate an interest in gaining or deepening understanding through asking questions, actively listening, or exploring new things.	Student occasionally demonstrates an interest in deepening understanding through asking questions, actively listening, and exploring new things.	Student consistently demonstrates an interest in deepening understanding through asking questions, actively listening, and exploring new things.	Student consistently demonstrates an interest in deepening understanding through asking questions, actively listening, and exploring new things. Student coaches or teaches peers to demonstrate curiosity and interest.
Optimism	No basis to judge.	Student is unable to overcome frustrations or setbacks quickly and does not believe that effort will improve his or her future.	Student occasionally overcomes frustrations and setbacks quickly. Student demonstrates some belief that effort will improve his or her future.	Student consistently overcomes frustrations and setbacks quickly and believes that effort will improve his or her future.	Student consistently overcomes frustrations and setbacks quickly and believes that effort will improve his or her future. Student teaches or coaches peers to demonstrate optimism and a sense of efficacy.
Grit	No basis to judge.	Student does not finish tasks and decreases effort when experiencing obstacles or failure.	Student occasionally finishes tasks and, at times, will try very hard even when experiencing obstacles or failure.	Student consistently finishes tasks and tries very hard even when experiencing obstacles or failure.	Student consistently finishes tasks and tries very hard even when experiencing obstacles or failure. Student teaches or coaches peers to persevere and demonstrate grit.
Social Intelligence	No basis to judge.	Student does not demonstrate respect for the feelings of others and is unable to find constructive solutions during conflicts with others.	Student inconsistently demonstrates respect for the feelings of others and, at times, is able to find constructive solutions during conflicts with others.	Student consistently demonstrates respect for the feelings of others and is able to find constructive solutions during conflicts with others.	Student consistently demonstrates respect for the feelings of others, is able to find constructive solutions during conflicts with others, and knows how to include others. Student teaches or coaches peers to consider the feelings of others, work toward constructive solutions to conflict, and include others when appropriate.

4

IMPLEMENTATION AND CASE STUDY EXAMPLES

General Principles and Application to a District New to SEL

Utility: This chapter provides a bridge between conceptual and applied implementation procedures, including recommendations from the authors, and case examples for districts without existing SEL or character programming. Methods to support communication between teachers and parents are discussed. Examples of how to use this Guide to improve assessment and reporting of emerging competencies through early learning standards and career and technical or college readiness are presented.

Maximizing Guide Resources: Case examples may prove helpful for administrators and task force members for a range of purposes, including demonstrating feasibility; promoting buy-in; offering a fuller, contextualized view of the process; and stimulating discussion of how your school or district is similar to or different from the examples. Key points may be worthwhile to extract as a resource to support teacher–parent conversations and conferences.

Key Takeaway and Reflection Points:

- School and district leadership teams are important to develop, to coordinate efforts and responsibilities effectively and efficiently.

- Supporting teachers' knowledge and ability to communicate comfortably with parents regarding your school or district's modified comment sections through training and supplemental resources is essential to involving parents and more effectively promoting student success.

IN THIS CHAPTER

As noted earlier, schools implementing an SEL or character report card will be following one of two main options, either deductive (based on already existing SEL or character programming) or inductive (based on a determination of the importance of highlighting and rating key SEL skills or character virtues, to be followed by SEL and character promotion programming). Because most schools will be using the latter option, an outline of inductive implementation procedures will be presented, followed by how to adapt those procedures for schools with SEL or character programming already in place. We begin with the most essential structure for implementation: the school leadership team for social, emotional, and character development (SECD). This is followed by a case study example of the inductive option. In Chapter 5, we focus on how to adapt the process in Chapter 4 for the deductive option, and in Chapter 6, we discuss the challenges typically faced during the process. In that chapter, we provide a focus on parent–teacher communication about SECD, an important part of any report card process, especially during parent–teacher conferences. That chapter concludes by illustrating how the Guide and its principles can be adapted to improve school and district assessment and reporting around emerging areas, using early learning standards and career and technical or college readiness as examples.

SCHOOL LEADERSHIP TEAMS: ESSENTIAL FOR ACCOMMODATING THE HEAD AND THE HEART DURING IMPLEMENTATION

Those engaged in the task of creating SEL or character report cards must recognize that anything new replaces something in existence, which had its own process of development and, usually, a comfort level among users. This is true even in the case of report card comment sections, which typically are not held in high esteem by teachers and are rarely found to be useful in school or district decision making. So considerable attention should be devoted to a process by which staff become familiar with SEL or character and are deeply involved in creating the new report card format.

Typically, a school leadership team for report card design and implementation (SLT but should be locally renamed) is essential because the school staff as a whole cannot usually accomplish the task. Sometimes, schools will pursue the report card change individually, but often, the process will be part of a multischool or districtwide initiative. In these cases, leaders of the SLTs will meet as a district leadership team (DLT) to ensure broad input into a coordinated solution.

In addition to the SLT carrying out the processes outlined in this Guide, there is an additional potential pitfall and tremendous opportunity that is part of the implementation of the SEL or character report card: the relationship with parents. The opportunity, as will be outlined below, is to create a relationship focused not only on students' academic performance but also on students' everyday skills and character. Although parents may need guidance, and some may need considerable assistance, these are areas that nearly all parents can relate to and, more so than most academic areas, exercise some positive influence over. The pitfalls come if teachers are not confident and comfortable in their knowledge and ability to talk to parents about SEL or character and its importance for their children, for education, and for college and career possibilities. Once comfortable with their knowledge base, teachers can then learn and be supported to speak confidently about the report card indicators. Part of that comfort and confidence is knowledge that when parents ask common but tough questions, such as "Where can I get help for my child?," the teachers are part of the solution but also that there are other resources and supports.

Ultimately, the SLTs will do the following:

1. They will assist in advocating for staff training in SEL skill or character development and supports to promote teacher abilities to discuss comments meaningfully.

2. They will encourage the distribution of helpful materials or other supports for educators and teachers. For example, the task force might develop a quick reference guide for teachers in assigning ratings (e.g., providing detailed definitions and behavior examples for each rated item or a reference guide on best practices for recognizing positive behaviors).

3. They will link ratings with methods of promoting SEL or character behaviors, referring to other parts of the Guide or outside resources (see the Resources section following Chapter 8) so that teachers and educators are better equipped to make discussions with parents meaningful and actionable for themselves and their children.

CASE STUDY EXAMPLE OF THE IMPLEMENTATION PROCESS

To illustrate an extended implementation process, the outline below is a case study of an urban school district that used an earlier version of this Guide to create a process of incorporating SEL and character systematically into report cards. The district used what we refer to as Option 1, starting with assessment and following to programming.

The process is outlined as a series of steps taking place over a three-year period of time. We follow the case example with an overview of the obstacles faced and overcome, highlight what turns out to be a major asset of having SEL and character on report cards (i.e., the change in teacher–parent conversations about students), and conclude with a summary of how the process differs in settings in which Option 2 is used, where SEL or character programming exists without the report card assessment component.

Step 1: Fall, Year 1: Became Familiar With Background Literature

- In-service on SEL, character, and school culture and climate for district administrators

Step 2: Fall–Spring, Year 1: Analyzed Current Report Cards; Proposed SEL or Character Options

- Created a focus group to analyze current report cards using the Guide and decide on changes to be made, including focus on SEL, character, or both
  - Focus group included representatives from all schools, with all grade levels represented (though not all grade levels for

all schools); teams included representatives of special subject areas (e.g., music, PE, art, and computers) and school support services (e.g., school counselors)

- Focus groups met six times over the course of four months to accomplish the following:
  - Reviewed literature on SEL and character as well as websites (see the Resources section following Chapter 8)
  - Found and reviewed examples of SEL (e.g., Anchorage, Alaska) and character (e.g., KIPP Academy, Montclair Kimberley Academy Character Reflections) report cards
  - Decided on a set of seven SEL skills that would be the focus for report card comment sections. SEL selected for two primary reasons:
    - Strong evidence linking the skills to academic performance
    - Concern that SEL skills could be more objectively assessed than character attributes (see Chapter 3 for more detailed discussion of differences between SEL and character definitions and skills examples)

Step 3: Spring, Year 1: Created Feasible Rating System

- Follow-up meeting with principals and district administrators to create school leadership teams (SLTs) to follow up on the details of creating a feasible rating system and an implementation plan. SLTs consisted of the following:
  - School administrator
  - Anti-bullying specialist
  - Guidance counselor
  - General education teachers representing half of the grades in the school (e.g., K–1 and 6–7)
  - Special education teacher
  - Special area teacher
- Teams selected a chairperson, who was also the SLT's representative or liaison to a district leadership team (DLT)
- Teams met twice per month, and all meetings had agendas, follow-up notes, and action items with responsibilities and deadlines or timelines to promote efficiency
- The SLTs had two primary goals:
  - Prepare for and pilot procedures for adapting report cards to include SEL
  - Develop a three-year SEL plan for the school, based on an assessment of current school practices and programs related to SEL and how best to help students develop skills in the seven designated SEL areas. This objective was intentionally delayed to focus on the pilot implementation of the report card process.

Step 4: Fall, Year 2: SLTs Deepened Knowledge; Inventoried Schools

- SLT's began to meet in order to do the following:
  - Build knowledge about SEL and school culture and climate by reading brief, user-friendly, well-established materials (e.g., Dunkelblau, 2009; Elias & Berkowitz, 2016) and viewing key websites (overview documents on SEL and character development assessment and implementation available at www.CASEL.org, www.character.org, and www.edutopia.org)
  - Explore practices already occurring in their individual schools, both through programming and otherwise, that were fostering SEL skills and character virtues

Step 5: Fall–Spring, Year 2: Engaged in District-Level Coordination and Planning to Create Indicators

- The DLT began to meet monthly, ultimately moving to twice per month to promote efficiency and consistency. The following sequence of meetings defines the remaining activities:

December: In-service for the DLT on SEL; each liaison created an "elevator pitch" for SEL (http://www.edutopia .org/blog/you-need-elevator-pitch-about-school-culture-and-climate-maurice-elias)

January: DLT reviewed the SEL report card skills and discussed rating possibilities; DLT liaisons encouraged their SLT members to develop elevator pitches for SEL and related skills

February: DLT created a grade level set of indicators of SEL skills capable of being observed by teachers and pilot-tested a rating system (students rated on a three-point scale: below, at, or above grade level expectations) based on case examples (see the case example sample in Table 4.1)

March: DLT refined rating task, determined who would be expected to provide ratings and when; created system of piloting the procedure in each SLT based on written case examples and then school-based examples (see case example "Aleah" below, with scoring from a teacher at the end)

April: Feedback from SLTs was used by the DLT to finalize the system and create PowerPoint presentations and sample activities to be used by SLTs to orient

SEL Area	SEL Behavior Indicators
Table 4.1 Sample Rating System from Case Study Example	
Self-Awareness & Self-Management	**Grade 3** • Can recognize and accurately label a range of emotions, including pride, surprise, frustration, loneliness, honesty, and fairness most of the time **with prompting** • Can connect feelings to situation in which they take place **with prompting**
Emotional Awareness Definition: Recognizes and labels one's emotions and connects feeling to situations	**Grade 4** • Can recognize and accurately label a range of emotions, including pride, surprise, frustration, loneliness, honesty, and fairness **most of the time** • Can connect feelings to situation in which they take place **with prompting** **Grade 5** • Can recognize and accurately label a range of emotions, including pride, surprise, frustration, loneliness, honesty, and fairness most of the time • Can connect feelings to situation in which they take place **without prompting**
Self-Awareness & Self-Management	**Grade 3** • Uses self-talk strategy to calm down when upset **with prompting** • Will tell the truth in a difficult situation **half** of the time • Can set and work toward goals in at least one area • Can follow through on multiple responsibilities **with prompting**
Emotion Regulation and Focus Definition: Use strategies to keep oneself calm and focus on goals	**Grade 4** • Uses self-talk strategy to calm down when upset **with prompting** • Will tell the truth in a difficult situation **most** of the time • Can set and work toward goals in at least one area • Can follow through on multiple responsibilities **with prompting** **Grade 5** • Uses self-talk strategy to calm down when upset **without prompting** • Will tell the truth in a difficult situation **most** of the time • Can set and work toward goals in at least one area • Can follow through on multiple responsibilities **without prompting**

Ratings Key:

Below grade level expectations

At grade level expectations

Above grade level expectations

staff members to SEL and report card ratings (e.g., videos used to orient staff at http://communities .newteachercenter.org/sel/pages/view?page=frame work and http://www.edutopia.org/blog/orienting-educators-sel-through-video-maurice-elias)

May: School staff pilot-tested the SEL report card rating format and provided feedback to SLTs; DLTs created final version based on feedback

June:	DLTs drafted support materials to go to parents to explain SEL skills and the rating system (e.g., materials to explain SEL to parents, in English and Spanish, at http://www.parenttoolkit.com/index.cfm?objectid=9214C140-32E9-11E4-AB0A0050569A5318)
June–August:	District administration integrated SEL into report cards and online database and data warehouse system used by the school

ALEAH, FIFTH GRADE

This case example, from school psychologist Leah Dembitzer, features Aleah, a verbal and talkative fifth-grader who does well in written and spoken academic work and is on grade level in math. Aleah is popular among classmates and always has peers to talk to and play with during free time. She has a wide circle of acquaintances with whom she interacts sporadically, rather than any close friends in the class. Aleah is quite adept at noticing how her peers are feeling and will seek out a classmate who is feeling sad to talk and make him or her feel better. Aleah likes to have her way and takes charge in group work by assigning tasks and directing the work. This has sometimes caused her classmates to complain. When this happens, Aleah apologizes and asks her classmates what they would like to do. When she finds schoolwork difficult, she tends to do a slapdash job in an attempt to get out of it as quickly as possible. However, when a teacher points out what is expected, Aleah accepts the feedback graciously and redoes the work. Given her strong academic capabilities, her teachers wish that she would try harder without prompting, but Aleah appears as though she cannot be bothered, putting in strong effort when encountering difficulty without feedback and/or redirection.

Aleah's ratings, based on the criteria defined in the sample rating system table above, are as follows:

Emotional awareness = Above grade level expectations

Emotion regulation/focus = Meets grade level expectations

Step 6: Summer–Fall, Year 3: Developed Three-Year Plan; Prepared Parents, Teachers, and Students

- The DLT met in summer, Year 3, to develop a three-year plan to systematically foster desired SEL skills, character virtues, and a positive culture and climate into their schools. Guidelines for this process are available from resources listed in this Guide, especially www.CASEL.org and www.character.org.
- In fall of Year 3, the DLT was involved with preparing parents and teachers for the SEL ratings and preparing students and parents for SEL-related discussions on the report card.

○ Teachers were concerned about being able to justify their ratings but realized that as long as they focused on their primary behavior samples (i.e., the specific contexts in which they observed students every day), they had no problem providing examples to parents of how they arrived at their ratings.

○ The DLT worked with teachers to develop tools to assist teachers in documenting examples of students exhibiting or lacking any of the seven SEL skills; this was offered to teachers as an aid but not as a mandated recording requirement.

○ Parents, who have a great interest in the character of their students as well as a great deal of responsibility for and influence on their children's behavior, welcomed the opportunity for a structured and ongoing discussion of their children's behavior.

○ Parents and teachers were able to engage in collaborative and ongoing conversations about how to respond to ratings. Three key principles were developed in this district that both relaxed teachers and reassured parents:

(1) When in doubt about a rating, round up (i.e., give the more positive rating).

(2) Allow for discrepancies in ratings by different raters, and note these patterns because they likely suggest skills are being applied differentially in different contexts.

(3) Interventions and concerns would be triggered by two consecutive marking periods of below-grade-level ratings, not one subpar marking period.

Step 7: Conducted Ongoing Monitoring and Implementation

• By spring of Year 3, there was ongoing monitoring of satisfaction on the part of parents and staff members with the rating process, with adjustments made as needed. The focus, however, shifted to the implementation of the three-year SEL, CD, and culture and climate improvement plans. Data from the report card ratings provide baseline data for interventions and are valuable as part of program evaluation.

5

IMPLEMENTATION WITH CASE STUDY EXAMPLES FOR SCHOOLS WITH CURRENT SEL OR CHARACTER PROGRAMMING

Utility: This chapter provides specific implementation considerations for schools with existing SEL and/or character programming. The emphasis, similar to Chapter 4, is on offering a bridge between conceptual and applied implementation procedures, with a focus on developing operational definitions for skills and traits emphasized by existing programming. Several evidence-based SEL and character-based programs are reviewed, including one program that combines the two.

Maximizing Guide Resources: Case examples may prove helpful for administrators and task force members for a range of purposes, including demonstrating feasibility; promoting buy-in; offering a fuller, contextualized view of the process; and stimulating discussion of how your school or district is similar to or different from the examples. Key points may be worthwhile to extract as a resource to support teacher–parent conversations and conferences.

Key Takeaway and Reflection Points:

- When SEL and/or character-based programming is in place, a deductive approach is needed in order to focus on the specific behaviors to be rated.

- After determining focal behaviors, implementation, in many ways, is a parallel process with what is described in Chapter 4 and involves deciding on the most appropriate rating system format and how to represent grade and age level expectations.

IN THIS CHAPTER

For schools and districts with an SEL or character education program in place or a defined approach to SECD, the task is somewhat different. In those situations, it is essential to match the assessment to the intervention. One common disadvantage of existing SEL and character assessments is their lack of alignment to one's specific program. However, using the approach in this Guide, it is possible for schools and districts to tailor report card indicators specifically to the interventions already in practice.

In the deductive situation, it is understood that in the process of selecting programs or approaches, decisions regarding focal skills and values have already been made. Thus, the development of an appropriate assessment method in the report card section must follow and align with programming. As a result, schools and districts should be able to shorten the implementation steps cycle described in Chapter 4. This will enable implementation decisions to occur at the end of year one, as opposed to year two. We recommend that schools and districts with existing programming review Chapter 4 if interested in getting a sense of the overall process, further understanding differences between these approaches, and/or approaching their own programming and focal skills and values with greater scrutiny.

CASE STUDY EXAMPLES

We share below five examples, two from schools that are using a character education approach or a values-focused approach and two from schools that have a set of identified SEL skills based in a curriculum. The last example is from a school infusing SEL skills throughout all subject areas without using a specific curriculum.

Open Circle: An SEL Curriculum Example

Open Circle (www.open-circle.org) is an evidence-based elementary-grades SEL curriculum. For Grade 3, Open Circle emphasizes *ten* key skills that are represented in their lessons and generalization structure:

1. Listening

2. Using nonverbal signals

3. Giving compliments

4. Including others

5. Cooperating

6. Dealing with tattling

7. Dealing with situations on one's own

8. Dealing with teasing

9. Speaking up

10. Encouraging others

Students rate themselves on each skill using a three-point scale (i.e., yes, no, and sometimes), and then respond to this prompt: "List the skills you would like to work on." Teachers create a class summary sheet based on the students' ratings, his or her own observations of the students, and a list of areas or skills that would benefit from greater focus. Individual schools are free to modify this format, choosing their own focal behaviors, modifying for different grade levels, and including reporting of these on the report cards formally or having informal conversations with parents based on these assessments.

I Can Problem Solve! (ICPS): An SEL Curriculum Example

Originally called Interpersonal Cognitive Problem Solving, ICPS (http://thinkingchild.com) began in the early 1970s and continues to be among the most widely used evidence-based SEL curricula, especially in preK through first grade. ICPS operationalizes (i.e., defines with specific, observable behaviors) a set of key skills that lend themselves to reporting on report cards, although to the knowledge of these authors, this has rarely taken place in practice. ICPS does provide its own assessment procedures, including such measures as the Preschool Interpersonal Problem Solving Test, the What Happens Next Game, and the Means-Ends Problem Solving Test. However, these are rarely used outside of a research context.

Some schools implementing ICPS have defined key skills in ways that lend themselves to implementation on report cards, using the procedures in this Guide. Here are some examples for preK and kindergarten:

- Understands the difference between *is* and *is not*
- Understands *same* and *different*
- Can consider what might or might not happen in interpersonal situations
- Can accurately group two interpersonal interactions that go together
- Can differentiate everyday actions that come before and after one another
- Recognizes and differentiates basic emotions (happy, sad, angry, proud, annoyed, and frustrated) in oneself (and, separately, in others)
- Can think of more than one way to solve a problem
- Listens attentively when spoken to by others

The ICPS approach focuses on important language distinctions as cognitive markers of problem-solving abilities. Ratings for preK and kindergarten level students would take into account the consistency of the behavior as well as whether it is present with prompting. For example, in preK, students faced with a problem may not be able to generate multiple solutions on their own, but in response to the question "What else can you try?," they can be expected to generate some ideas, especially by the end of preK. Integrating SEL indicators consistent with the ICPS program into report cards would help schools to prioritize expectations at each grade level and have a way of systematically documenting progress in ways that do not require external assessments or scoring and that are tailored to their specific programs.

An SEL Infusion Example

A suburban public school for Grades 3–6 focusing on the theme of responsibility identified two main areas in which it wanted to infuse key behaviors in all parts of the curriculum. It then identified the focal behaviors related to each area and had teachers integrate them into lesson plans and everyday classroom and school routines. After implementing this approach for several years, a decision was made to operationalize the skills into the school report card. After engaging in the process outlined in the Guide, it arrived at the following system:

RESPONSIBILITY FOR LEARNING

- Participates and cooperates in a group setting
- Uses time effectively
- Listens and follows directions
- Completes class work
- Completes and returns homework on time
- Produces neat and organized work

RESPONSIBILITY FOR BEHAVIOR

- Displays self control
- Follows classroom rules
- Follows school rules
- Accepts and respects authority
- Accepts responsibility for own behavior
- Respects rights and property of others

Each behavior was rated for each child and each marking period (a trimester in this school) via a consensus of faculty who worked with the child in academic areas. So this might include input from basic-skills instructors, in-class support personnel, or gifted-and-talented teachers. The rating format selected was ✓+, ✓, and ✓−, denoting above expectations, satisfactory, and needing improvement. This system was used rather than a more objective or developmental standard because faculty wanted to evaluate each student over time using their own their own abilities and potential as a baseline. Such an approach is especially well suited to small schools, schools working in small units, and other situations where educators have ample opportunities to confer about a given student to arrive at a consensus. Such areas as "using time effectively" and "accepts responsibility for own behavior" clearly can vary considerably for students, depending on their age and abilities. Where instruction is differentiated—including for SECD, as it was infused in this school—assessment requires corresponding flexibility.

Character Counts! A Character Program Example

Many schools use a character education approach, and among these, one of the most common is Character Counts! In this model, the focus is on developing what is referred to as the six pillars of character: trustworthiness, respect, responsibility, fairness, caring, and citizenship. Most character programs are typified by articulating a set of values, virtues, character attributes, or the like and then building programming around them. What is less typical is to systematically assess how students are doing with regard to character development as part of the report card.

One independent K–12 school in the Northeast worked to operationalize its key values following the procedure outlined in this Guide. Although it did not have to begin by deciding on which aspects of character to emphasize, it still had to engage in discussions about how to assess the values focused on in programming. Two examples below reflect its decisions at the secondary level.

RESPONSIBILITY

- Do the right thing when no one is looking
- Accountable for my words and behavior
- Take care of my things
- Respect others' things
- Work hard at remembering what is required of me as a member of the school community

FAIRNESS

- Share materials with classmates
- Take turns
- Speak respectfully to others even when it is hard to do so
- Act respectfully toward others even when it is hard to do so
- Treat others the way I would like to be treated

RATING SCALE

- 5 = Exemplar with strong consistency
- 4 = Positive role model
- 3 = Significant positive and negative qualities
- 2 = Poor role model
- 1 = Altogether lacking

Note: For each rating, staff is asked to provide at least one incident or example in support of that rating.

As you review this example, you may well disagree with how the values are operationalized, with how the rating scale is defined, or both. That, in part, is the point of seeing diverse examples and engaging in a school-focused process. This school had strong consensus about what to look for and how to rate. Further, the rating and wording were designed to take into account having students also self-rate. To impose a more "objective" or "validated" values scale that did not reflect the indicators most important to the school community would lead to problematic ratings and a disconnect with the existing programming.

Touchstones: A Character and SEL (SECD) Example

Another approach to establishing focal values is to create "touchstones" that represent what the school stands for and to define these values and the corresponding behaviors. They typically include an overall motto, followed by supportive statements that become focal behaviors for rating at age-appropriate levels. Here are three examples, with focal behaviors for assessment italicized:

BETSY ROSS SCHOOL (K–8)

Motto: Expect More, Learn More, Be More

Touchstones:

- We are *respectful, supportive, responsible, honest, hardworking, courteous* and *kind.*
- Our efforts create an environment that is *safe, inviting, and productive.*
- We have *confidence* in ourselves and our achievements.

BENJAMIN FRANKLIN ELEMENTARY SCHOOL (K–5)

Motto: The Franklin Promise

Touchstones:

- At Franklin, we *learn and laugh together.*
- We *respect each other* by using *kind words and actions.*
- We *take responsibility for our own learning and behavior*, even when no one is watching.
- At Franklin, we *celebrate* each other's *differences and accomplishments.*

CROSSROADS SCHOOL (K–8)

Motto: If you can imagine it, you can achieve it.

Touchstones:

- We *honor* and *respect* individual differences.
- We *take responsibility for* our *learning* and our *actions.*
- We *communicate* with each other in a *caring, honest,* and *positive* way.
- We learn with a *smile* and a *joyful attitude.*

From these existing touchstones, which schools will have previously established, the next step becomes to operationalize the behaviors and create rating systems. These conversations sometimes lead to revisiting the touchstones so as to clarify or to make them more readily translated into specific, observable behaviors. In the case of the Betsy Ross School, meeting the spirit of the touchstones also necessitates school climate assessment to ensure that the kind of environment pledged is being perceived by students and staff. Further, the touchstone regarding confidence in achievements connects to creating portfolios of artifacts of various projects, emanating not only from classes but also from clubs and teams. In addition, staff reconsiders assignments when the presentation of artifacts becomes important (versus focusing only on a grade for an assignment). This, in part, comes to broaden and deepen the definition of the school motto. Similarly, at Franklin, the emphasis on learning and laughing together and on mutual respect and celebration leads to metrics beyond those of individual student attributes. Students' roles as assets to others become important to document, as does the collective influence of these actions on the school culture and climate.

SUMMARY AND IMPLICATIONS

These are examples of the generative process that unfolds in practice when schools seek to operationalize SEL or character efforts already in place into their report card systems. The general principles that settings using the deductive approach have to follow to get to the point of operationalizing their efforts are as follows:

1. Deciding, among the many possible behaviors that could be rated, which ones will be the focus

2. Deciding on a rating system format

3. Deciding on how to represent grade or age level expectations.

6

MOST FREQUENT CHALLENGES ADDRESSED AND OVERCOME

Reassuring and Involving Parents and Aligning to Early Childhood Education and Career and Technical Education Goals

Utility: Frequently encountered challenges in implementation are discussed in this chapter to better prepare educators for optimal implementation and sustainability. Specific focus on parent–teacher interactions is included.

Maximizing Guide Resources: Common challenges may help your team anticipate barriers and promote discussion around ways to be most efficient and effective in implementation. Consider distributing these challenges to key staff (e.g., school or district leadership teams) to stimulate discussion of those anticipated to be most relevant and how they may be best overcome in your school or district. Parts of this chapter regarding parent–teacher conversations and conferences may be extracted to provide a reference guide for teachers on key themes and techniques to keep in mind.

Key Takeaway and Reflection Points:

- Make clear what skills and behaviors are most important, what specifically to look for in identifying them, how to direct parent focus, and what can mitigate many common challenges.

- Feasibility and congruence with current programming as well as school and community culture may also serve to reduce the likelihood of serious impediments resulting from potential challenges.

IN THIS CHAPTER

Regardless of whether a school is using the inductive or deductive approach, there is a common set of challenges that the process encounters. Articulating these challenges and the actions taken to surmount them in the past allows those now implementing SECD assessment to better overcome them. These include the following:

- *Time will be needed for teachers to successfully input data and grades.* School administration must work with teachers to provide the necessary time, usually as part of ongoing professional development or common planning times. One school had early dismissal once each quarter, and teachers remained to collaborate on the report card ratings.

- *Items and indicators will need to be carefully worded to minimize subjectivity.* Teacher review of items accomplishes this goal.
- *Teachers should be focused on rating what they most clearly see, rather than what they hear about secondhand or see only on occasion (e.g., behavior in lunchrooms).* Establishing clear parameters about the basis for ratings addresses this concern, though drift is often natural. The discipline involved in focusing one's ratings also leads teachers to realize when their impressions about students are being influenced by secondhand information.
- *Schools should determine whether to have average ratings and how to account for discrepancies among raters based on situation-specific behavior by students.* Schools either report multiple ratings and/or use open-ended comments for the purpose of explaining situational discrepancies, which usually provide important information about student competencies.
- *Teacher fears (e.g., "Are we qualified to give opinions?") will need to be addressed.* Remind teachers that they used to give opinions on the largely baseless drop-down comments sections and that sticking to what they observe gives them unparalleled qualifications. Indeed, they are not giving their opinions about SEL any more than they do in math and reading; they are giving their professional observations.
- *Schools need to ensure that character ratings are not viewed as indicators of a child's enduring personality but rather how the child acts in the particular situation being rated.* This requires teachers to become more aware of situational differences in behavior and to embrace the notion that all children can improve their SECD. Hence, you may notice that we eschew the use of the word *trait* in this Guide because traits tend to connote inborn and unchangeable aspects of personality. This does not reflect current views of SECD.
- *Teachers and staff will need to deal with any discomfort in having SEL-related conversations with parents, and schools should provide the practice and support for them to do so.* This is addressed in detail below, as it is often the cause of greatest hesitation and encompasses many of the specific challenges noted above.

The latter point, concerning parent–teacher conversations, creates a powerful dynamic that can be crucial to the ultimate success of the SEL or character report card process. Helping teachers and parents (and students) adequately prepare for those conversations and their implications is essential, and considerations in doing so are presented next. This is followed by showing how SEL or character report card assessment can and should be aligned with emerging movements and trends in education, with early childhood and career and technical education being salient examples at the moment.

GUIDING PARENT–TEACHER CONVERSATIONS AND CONFERENCES: HOW TO USE SEL OR CHARACTER REPORT CARDS IN A FEEDBACK PROCESS WITH PARENTS

As academic standards change, the challenges of presenting them to parents multiply. The current basis for standards in most American schools, the Common Core State Standards, attempts to provide new levels of rigor and specificity across language arts and mathematics, in particular. Regardless, there is a clear trend for states, education departments, and ministries of education to use increasingly detailed and technical frameworks for guiding education.

These efforts create communication challenges, particularly for parents who are themselves not products of higher education, intimidated by schools, and/or for whom English is not a primary or comfortable language. Yet these parents share with all parents a desire for their students' educational success, a value for education, and a desire to help. The addition of SEL or character considerations to report cards provides a truly revolutionary opportunity to engage all parents in a feasible partnership in their children's education.

Specifically, having these ratings present systematically on all report cards, rated for all marking periods, accomplishes the following goals:

- Identifies areas of strength and areas in need of improvement that parents should know about
- Frames parent–teacher conversations in terms of an alliance in building a child's SECD, for which each party has an indispensible role
- Serves as a springboard for planning interventions and monitoring progress
- Allows for the involvement of the child in a cooperative project— his or her social-emotional and character development— alongside teachers, other educators, and parents
- Makes clear connections between the skills assessed and future success in academics and life

Identify Strengths and Needs

All students need encouragement, and SEL or character assessment provides an opportunity to speak about strengths alongside areas needing improvement. The framing of the latter is important, as well, in that everyone can improve aspects of their SEL and/or character, regardless of how accomplished (or not) they might be. So these conversations should begin with a discussion of strengths and then move into areas of improvement. It is essential for educators to be aware that the feedback to parents with regard to SEL or character attributes tells parents how their children appear to those in school. It does not define for the parent how the child *is* but, rather, provides feedback about the child in the school context as well as the consistency of the behavior of the child within various school contexts. As noted earlier, guidelines to follow include rounding upward when there is a doubt about a rating on a boundary between two scores and not being quick to push the panic button with parents regarding SEL or character indicators that are below expectations for a single marking period. Obviously, where these are linked to serious behavior problems, prompt action will be needed, but this will have been triggered by those actions, not by seeing negative SEL or character indicators on the report card for the first time.

Create an Alliance to Build Social-Emotional and Character Competencies

The conversation then moves to what the school is doing to help improve a child's SECD, framed in the broader context of overall schoolwide efforts to create a positive school culture and climate and the need for a developmental approach to skill-building. This sets the stage for realistic expectations, as opposed to the notion that all possible areas of improvement will be resolved by the end of the academic year.

Plan Interventions

Then, priorities must be identified. One or two areas for improvement should be the focus for both home and school. Specific ideas and/or resources should be provided to parents regarding what they can do to help. These often will involve changes in the family routines, changes in parent–child conversations, discussions about discipline practices, and focal situations when particular skills are important in home life. The concept of "catch kids being good" can be amended to "catch kids showing skills and character," and parents can be alerted to how to give specific praise at these times. Schools may consider providing specific guidance (in various languages, as needed) for parents as well as designating a parent intervention coordinator who can discuss progress monitoring in between marking periods. Progress monitoring allows for adjustments in intervention plans as needed and allows parents to feel supported and guided in what may be an unfamiliar process for many of them. There is an emerging technology of SEL- and character-related electronic games that provide assessment and skill-building opportunities (e.g., for children and adolescents).

Involve the Child

Before anything is implemented, the conversation should also include a discussion of who will speak to the child about his or her SECD progress and any potential planned interventions. It is crucial that children understand, from the earliest age, that how they act toward others in various situations will determine much of their potential life accomplishments, often in ways that can override their intellectual and other abilities. When and where will these conversations take place? How can parents explain (or be helped to explain) what they will be doing differently at home and why? (There are excellent materials on SEL and its applications in home contexts—including academics—across the developmental span at NBC-Universal's Parent Toolkit, http://bit.ly/1wtXuT5, in English and Spanish.) What materials can be given to the child to help build his or her awareness of his or her areas in need of improvement? (There is a growing number of relevant books and computer-based games for this purpose; www.zoougame.com, thesocialexpress.com, and rippleeffects. com are three examples at the time of this writing, and www.edutopia.org typically learns about and curates updates.) Parents and students need to know when and how to approach the school if they are uncomfortable with how interventions are going or perceive difficulties in between monitoring periods. School-based professionals have the expertise to provide guidance and make adjustments in these circumstances.

Reiterate the Rationale: Skills, Character, and Career, College, and Life Success

The culminating and summary point for all conversations—as well as the reason these conversations will actually be ongoing—is their importance for children. Educators, parents, and children must be clear that social-emotional competencies and character matter as much—not more but as much—for success in school, careers, college, and life as their academic competencies. In fact, they are essential *for* that success. Why is the school now starting to focus on this more? Why are parents working on it at home? They are doing so because they care and because it matters. There is nothing punitive about this. Having an opportunity on the report card for feedback about how social-emotional competencies and character are playing out in the school creates the conversations of caring about children that they need to become the best that they can be.

Changing the nature of parent–teacher–student conversations is an ongoing process because the conversation is influenced by changing trends in education. SEL and character competencies are relevant to any educational program, innovation, or fad because those competencies are salient to whatever happens in the interpersonal and relational environment of schools. However, it will be important to explicate the connections so that they are visible and clear even to those with relatively little knowledge about SEL or character virtues. Below, we show how this is happening currently as schools align SEL and character to growing initiatives in early learning and career and technical education goals (with each going by similar names in different locations, e.g., early childhood education, preK–3 education, career and college goals, and STEM and technical education goals).

APPLICATIONS TO EARLY LEARNING

Many states are participating in such initiatives as the Race to the Top Early Learning Challenge. In this work, many are guided by the domains of readiness defined by the National Research Council in 2008 in *Early Childhood Assessment: Why, What, and How?* The domains of readiness are language and literacy development, cognition and general knowledge, approach toward learning, physical well-being and motor development, and social-emotional development.

Approaches toward learning are often linked with the Common Core concept of habits of mind, which are ways children are supposed to approach learning situations; these are clearly complementary to social-emotional skills. Ultimately, individual states, districts, and schools must decide on exactly what, among many possibilities, they will focus on. Below are examples from New Jersey and Oregon.

New Jersey Early Learning Standards

In New Jersey, the state DOE decided to focus on approaches to learning, related to habits of mind. The approaches are defined as follows:

1. Attention

2. Engagement and persistence

3. Problem solving

4. Creativity and motivation

5. Flexibility and inventiveness

As of this writing, New Jersey is in the process of operationalizing these skills with regard to age level expectations, beginning at preschool and moving eventually through third grade. Using the processes in this Guide, these approaches can be operationalized and put into report cards or related reporting formats. The use of our process would likely yield separate indicators for engagement (which is more linked to sustained focus on tasks and activities) and persistence (which may include resistance to distraction and ability to return to tasks), creativity (which involves innovative use of materials and expression of ideas) and motivation (which may include taking initiative in various school-related contexts), and flexibility (which can connote openness to doing things in alternative ways) and inventiveness (which would have to be clearly differentiated from creativity, perhaps along the idea of connecting inventiveness to tangible items and creativity to ideas or language).

The necessity of creating a format that will be shared with parents and rated by teachers based on their everyday observations of their students fosters clarity with regard to how skills are operationalized and differentiated at age levels. Optimal use will result from the time taken to discuss and arrive at these consensually in one's context; use of standardized indicators is less likely to yield satisfactory utilization and results at this stage of the field's development.

Oregon Kindergarten Readiness

Oregon has focused on operationalizing readiness skills for kindergarten students. Among the SEL-related skills it has identified are the following indicators:

1. Observes rules and follows direction without requiring repeated reminders

2. Sees own errors in a task and corrects them

3. Willing to share toys or other things with other children when playing; does not fight or argue with playmates in disputes over property

4. Responds to instructions and then begins an appropriate task without being reminded

Its original plan is to rate these skills along the dimensions of never, rarely, sometimes, frequently, and always. (*Recommendations for a Statewide Oregon Kindergarten Readiness Assessment* is available at www.elccollaborative.org/assessment/77-kindergarten-entry-assessment.html.)

However, the approach recommended in this Guide would likely lead to other ways of operationalizing these behaviors. For example, separation might be required for "observes rules" and "follows directions." What constitutes a *repeated* reminder? Should there be a differentiation between seeing errors and correcting them? Perhaps a rubric approach might work best, starting with children who neither see nor correct errors (with or without prompting) and ending with those who both see and correct errors. Indicator 3 contains four separate behaviors that would merit discussion so as to create comfortable ratings and parental feedback. Similarly, the differentiation of responding to instructions and starting the subsequent task may need to be clarified as well as what degree of reminder would be acceptable (taking into account what is decided for Indicator 1).

CAREER AND TECHNICAL EDUCATION GOALS

As states define career and technical education goals, career readiness standards, and related areas, they are implicitly entering the realm of social-emotional and character development. In reviewing sets of standards for Grades 4–12, one finds that a combination of SEL skills and character dispositions are part of many of the standards. Note that typically, these standards were not arrived at with an explicit reference to SEL or character development but rather were derived from career and technical education literature and best practices. They were also not intended to be operationalized for report card ratings—something that we discuss below as diminishing their effectiveness and clarity. Reviewing standards from the District of Columbia and states such as Colorado, Pennsylvania, New York, and New Jersey as well as the National Board for Professional Teaching Standards, the following are representative of interpersonal standards with clear connections to SEL and character.

1. Act as a responsible and contributory citizen to one's classroom, school, and community

2. Apply skills that you have appropriately for situations you are involved with

3. Show positive health and financial habits

4. Communicate effectively and justify your communications as appropriate

5. Consider the consequences of your decision making

6. Display creativity and innovation

7. Effectively get information needed or new information as necessary

8. Show problem solving and persistence in the face of obstacles

9. Display ethical behavior and leadership

10. Set personal, academic, educational, career, and contribution or service goals

11. Use time productively

12. Work in increasingly diverse or multicultural teams

For these standards to have genuine influence on students' college and career paths, they would benefit from being explicated on school report cards. For those seeking to operationalize these standards in a reporting format that would be shared with students and parents, it becomes essential to follow the principles in this Guide for creating report card (or at least report card–ready) indicators. For example, in Point 1 above, what entails responsibility and contributory citizenship would need to be differentiated as well as developmentally defined. Point 2 is a bit general, 7 is relatively specific, and 9 contains two overlapping areas that likely should not be combined into one, unless the standard is about ethical leadership.

Moreover, it is often the case that standards such as the above define the end point. We might expect that by high school graduation, we would want all students to be able to be competent in all of these skill areas. Clearly, that outcome would enhance college and career readiness. The challenge becomes articulating meaningful developmental benchmarks. Perhaps they are not year by year. Ultimately, those doing the rating need to be able to discuss what they can see and rate that relates to the standards. Guidance that comes from state policies and standards should be exactly that: guidance. Responsible professionals at the school and district levels, especially in a spirit of sharing with colleagues from surrounding schools and districts, can arrive at viable indicators that then should become part of the report card system. Doing so ensures they will merit sustained attention on the part of educators, students, parents, and the wider community. Imagine a student being able to bring such a report card to prospective employers!

SUMMARY

The principles articulated in this Guide are being used and can be used in a variety of school contexts in which social-emotional and character development is implicitly or explicitly being assessed. Ultimately, schools and districts need to have focused discussions about what they value, what they would like teachers to be looking for, and what they want parents to be focused on. The number of relevant skills and dispositions is well beyond specific assessment. Hence, informed choices must be made to create feasible assessment and reporting systems. Where relevant, the indicators chosen should be aligned with ongoing approaches to social-emotional and character development in one's school. Having this systematic feedback about the students' competencies, in turn, will help those accepting them at the next grade level or in employment or higher education contexts to know more about them than simply their academic grades. They will know about the whole child and the kinds of skills that foster contribution and success.

7

CHECKLIST OF IMPORTANT CONSIDERATIONS

Utility: We provide one method for briefly reviewing an adapted report card comment section based on how it aligns with some of the key considerations outlined in this Guide.

Maximizing Guide Resources: Consider providing this checklist to members of the school or district leadership teams to provide a brief assessment of your adapted comment section and potentially highlight areas that would benefit from revisions or additions.

Key Takeaway and Reflection Points:

- Does your adapted comment section address each relevant point on the checklist? If not, has this point been determined to be not relevant, or is it being addressed in another way?

Below, we provide a method for reviewing the process you are using to create an adapted report card comment section. With this checklist, you can assess your progress in aligning what you are doing with some of the key considerations outlined in this Guide.

AREA TO CHECK: SCHOOL AND/OR COMMUNITY MISSION, GOALS, AND VALUES ARE RELATED TO THE ELEMENTS OF SEL AND CHARACTER VIRTUES EMPHASIZED IN RATINGS

- This can be accomplished by doing the following:
  - Forming a task force and/or series of work groups with a strong understanding of the school and community mission and culture in selecting SEL and character virtues and skills to rate and emphasize
  - Surveying administration, teachers, and staff to determine the most essential elements of SEL and character virtues for your district or school

AREA TO CHECK: ITEMS BEING RATED ARE CLEARLY DEFINED

- This can be accomplished by doing the following:
  - Aligning each item to a specific, observable behavior
  - Linking items being rated to several specific, observable behaviors to serve as indicators (e.g., included near the item, in a key, as part of a rubric, or in separate reference material that is readily accessible to raters)

AREA TO CHECK: ITEMS ARE DEVELOPMENTALLY APPROPRIATE

- This can be accomplished by doing the following:
  - Using the "SEL Skill Trajectory" (online supplement available at http://resource.corwin.com/EliasReportCard) to appropriately select skills for each grade level or grouping
  - Using the "Common Characteristics of Student Behavior" (Tables 3.2 and 3.3) to ensure that items are aligned with the behaviors one would expect to see from students in a given grade level or grouping
  - Eliciting feedback from staff or pilot-testing the extent to which the student population aligns with developmental mappings created for the ratings

AREA TO CHECK: ITEMS THAT CHANGE ACROSS GRADE LEVELS OR GROUPINGS ARE LINKED AND REPRESENTATIVE OF ONGOING SKILL DEVELOPMENT

- This can be accomplished by doing the following:
  - Utilizing the "Developmentally Adapted SEL Likert Rating System: Progression by Grade Level" (online supplement available at http://resource.corwin.com/EliasReportCard) as a reference to demonstrate how skills can build on one another to support acquisition
  - Utilizing the "SEL Skill Trajectory" (online supplement available at http://resource.corwin.com/EliasReportCard) to identify skills that build on one another as grade levels or groupings ascend
  - Investigating the conceptual mapping and flow of items as grade levels ascend to determine if more complex skills expected at higher grade levels are adequately addressed and broken down at lower grade levels into the components needed for the more complex skill to be demonstrated

AREA TO CHECK: SUPPORT IS PROVIDED TO TEACHERS OR RATERS TO PROMOTE ACCURACY IN RATINGS AND ABILITY TO MAXIMIZE MEANINGFUL FEEDBACK

- This can be accomplished by doing the following:
  - Ensuring staff have a basic understanding of SEL and/or character virtues before introducing any report card revisions or revision-related tasks
  - Conducting training or pilot testing involving defining the SEL skills and/or character virtues intended to be rated and how they may manifest behaviorally; offering instruction and differentiation as to how ratings should be provided; exploring SEL- and character-based concepts, background of the evidence supporting these skills, methods for facilitating parent contact and having meaningful conversation around ratings, and more
  - Distributing quick reference guides to provide additional criteria (e.g., amount of time or number of times the behavior needs to be demonstrated to support each rating level), behavioral indicators and manifestations (e.g., specific, observable behaviors for each rated item and example scenarios in which this behavior could emerge), and/or further definitions of an item or skill grouping
  - Discussing the rating process in teacher and staff meetings, particularly those working with the same grade level or grouping to promote consistency and troubleshoot issues and discrepancies

AREA TO CHECK: PROVIDE INFORMATION ON RATINGS TO SUPPORT PARENT UNDERSTANDING AND INVESTMENT

- This can be accomplished by doing the following:
  - Providing introductory materials about the benefits and rationale of SEL and character virtues and the rating system (e.g., promotes consistency and communication around behaviors relevant to competence in academic, workplace, and various other relevant life situations)
  - Highlighting the manner in which information gathered from ratings will be used to inform programming, interventions, classroom lessons, or otherwise, as appropriate
  - Identifying opportunities for parents to discuss ratings with teachers and provide ways they can receive support or feedback on addressing relevant behaviors at home
  - Reviewing parents' responses to report card conversations about SEL or character virtues feedback for their students, responses to materials, and follow-through on skill building or other suggestions to help their students

8

LITERATURE REVIEW ON PREVIOUS STUDIES RELATED TO "THE OTHER SIDE" OF THE REPORT CARD

Utility: We provide a more in-depth view of the literature leading to the rationale for "the other side of the report card." Data-driven decision-makers, those skeptical about the process, and others who would benefit from a more thorough understanding of the literature behind the movement are potential target audiences for this resource.

Despite the widespread use of report card comments on students' behavior or work habits, we have only been able to identify two other research teams that have empirically studied their use and value. The first team, led by Stephen J. Friedman, conducted two studies. Friedman and Frisbie (1995) analyzed report cards from fifty-nine elementary schools, forty-eight middle schools, and seventy high schools to identify the characteristics of information on report cards. While most elementary school report cards had space for teacher-written comments, almost all of the high school report cards relied exclusively on drop-down menus for comments. Middle school report cards used both methods about evenly. When menus for comments were used, teachers were usually able to select only two out of as many as eighty different comments for each student.

The second study by Friedman and colleagues sought to better understand how report card comments related to student performance. Friedman, Valde, and Obermeyer (1998) examined a middle school of 475 students where its report cards allowed teachers to select up to two comments from a menu of eighty-two comments. They discovered that these teachers were more likely to use negative comments to explain low grades than positive comments to explain high grades, even though teachers were most likely to assign positive comments. Friedman and colleagues have not conducted any further research on this topic and are unaware of similar work (G. A. Valde, personal communication, February 10, 2012).

The second research team, headed by Angela Lee Duckworth, developed New York City's first-ever character report card at the KIPP network of charter schools (Tough, 2012). The character report card is distributed to students twice yearly and includes twenty-four indicators that measure seven strengths identified through the positive-psychology literature: zest, grit, self-control, social intelligence, gratitude, optimism, and curiosity. These indicators are used to calculate a "character point average" to complement the more traditional grade point average (Tough, 2012). While the KIPP report card is being studied empirically, no peer-reviewed studies have been published as of this writing.

THE SEL REPORT CARD INDICATOR STUDIES

Building on the Friedman and KIPP work, the SEL report card indicator (SEL-RCI) studies focused specifically on the influence of social-emotional learning on academic performance and the extent to which this was being captured in existing report card comments. The initial phase of the SEL-RCI addressed three research questions:

Q1: Are the CASEL 5 dimensions of SEL represented well by report card comments? What other dimensions seem to be represented?

Q2: What is the relationship of report card comments to different levels of academic performance, different demographic groups, and different grade levels?

Q3: How well do comments on student report cards adhere to SEL theory?

To explore these research questions, we conducted three studies: The Elementary School SEL-RCI Study (Moceri & Elias, 2015), the Middle School SEL-RCI Study (Kemp, Moceri, & Elias, 2015), and the High School SEL-RCI Study (Moceri, Elias, Fishman, Epstein, & Selby, 2015). All three studies tackled the research questions using different approaches for three reasons:

1. A different research team within our lab conducted each study and each one placed different emphases on the three research questions.

2. The report card format was different for each study, which meant that the methodology had to be modified to fit the structure and presentation of the report cards. (For instance, teachers in the elementary school study could select as many comments as they desired from their list of twenty-four possibilities, whereas teachers in the high school study could only select up to two comments from their list of twenty-five possible behavior comments.)

3. As each of our research teams completed their studies, our knowledge about what the SEL-RCI could mean and could accomplish grew. So each study informed the next one.

The studies are presented in the order that they were conducted.

THE MIDDLE SCHOOL SEL-RCI STUDY

The emphasis of the Middle School SEL-RCI Study (Kemp et al., 2015) was to closely examine who receives what type of comments. More specifically, we were interested in the relationship of race or ethnicity and gender to behavioral comments and letter grades. This led us to examine report cards from three middle schools in a large suburban district in New Jersey. Each school had about 1,000 students. The district provided us with report cards and school records for the 2007–2008 academic year. Report cards for this school included behavioral comments and academic letter grades. School records included the students' grade level (i.e., sixth, seventh, and eighth grade), gender, and race or ethnicity. We limited our analyses to Hispanic, black, and white students, as the other ethnic groups were not large enough for comprehensive statistical analyses. From these students, we randomly selected 200 students from each grade level. Of the 600 students, 54.7% were female (n = 328), 64.7% were white (n = 388), 19.7% were black (n = 118), and 15.7% were Hispanic (n = 94). These demographics were relatively similar to the district-level data.

Teachers chose behavioral comments from a list of sixteen possibilities, with a limit of three comments per class per marking period. Similar to the other SEL-RCI studies, the report card did not provide teachers with any categories or groupings for the comments. One SEL-experienced undergraduate research assistant (the lead author of this study, who is now certified as a school psychologist), one graduate student who was the co-principal investigator of the SEL-RCI (Dominic C. Moceri, the third author of this book), and the principal investigator of the SEL-RCI (Maurice J. Elias, the first author of this book) dichotomized the comments into positive (e.g., reveals imagination and creativity or shows evidence of consistent effort) and negative (e.g., assumes an indifferent attitude or does not follow directions) categories. The total number of each type of comment category was added together across all classes separately for each quarter to yield positive and negative comment scores. (Comments were not coded into CASEL 5 categories as that distinction was not part of the literature at the time of this study.)

We found several significant differences by race or ethnicity and gender for comments and letter grades based on analysis of variance and nonparametric statistical tests. Black, Hispanic, and male students received more negative comments, fewer positive comments, and worse letter grades than their white and female peers. The findings provided important suggestive caution to school personnel about the possible operation of rater bias, the need to address enduring behavioral discrepancies among subgroups in schools, and the importance of simplifying rating systems to allow them to be amenable to data analysis and, therefore, to be sources of ongoing feedback for schools.

THE HIGH SCHOOL SEL-RCI STUDY

The emphasis of the High School SEL-RCI Study (Moceri et al., 2015) was to determine whether the behavioral ratings and comments sections of the report card related to student performance in a manner consistent with SEL theory. SEL skills, as captured in report card comments, should be associated with fewer attendance problems, higher letter grades, and higher standardized test scores.

We worked with an ethnically diverse, large high school in New Jersey in a district that was the combination of two communities, in part for reasons of desegregation. This school had an enrollment of approximate 2,000 students. Approximately 20% of the students qualified for a free or reduced lunch. Over 50% of the students were black and over 33% were white. The school provided us with report cards and school records for their 2007–2008 academic school year for Grades 9–11.

Report cards included behavioral comments, academic letter grades, and attendance variables. School records included grade level, gender, race or ethnicity, free- or reduced-lunch status, and standardized test scores. Within all these factors, we had to make some decisions about which students we would focus on. We included all white and black students who took a yearlong language and literature course (LA) and/or a yearlong math course (MA). LA and MA courses were chosen because these subject areas have standardized test scores in the state of New Jersey, and most high school students take these classes. We excluded students of other ethnicities (about 10%, as combining them into one group could be highly misleading) and students who had an individualized education program. Additionally, as initial analyses revealed that only four out of 239 students who qualified for a free or reduced lunch were white, those four students were eliminated from the dataset to protect their privacy and to prevent improper generalization. Using the above criteria, we analyzed the report cards of 1,243 students, with approximately half being female, about 58% being black, and almost 20% qualifying for a free or reduced lunch (about a third of the black sample). Students were evenly split across grade levels.

On the report card, teachers rated students' behaviors by choosing up to two behavior comments per class per quarter from a list of twenty-five options. The comment list was highly representative of those used in other high school drop-down menus. The report card did not provide teachers with any categories or groupings for the comments. We coded the comments to determine how well they matched the CASEL 5 conceptualization of SEL skills. A three-phase process determined that there were ten comment categories, which were divided into SEL and non-SEL categories. The SEL categories were self-management and "other SEL," which represented the other four core CASEL 5 competencies. Fewer than half (n = 10) of the twenty-five comments were SEL-related, which was not surprising because SEL was not a consideration in the formation of comment categories. The non-SEL comment categories were academic, attendance, improvement, and preparedness. Both SEL and non-SEL categories were divided into positive and negative groups.

Black students, male students, and students qualifying for a free or reduced lunch had more negative comments and lower standardized test scores than their white, female, and non-lunch-qualifying peers. Additionally, black students had fewer positive comments and lower letter grades than whites. These findings were similar to those found in the Middle School SEL-RCI Study.

Comments were not a good predictor of absences, but negative comments were often associated with more tardies. In particular, students with negative self-management comments in language and math courses were tardy approximately two additional times over the academic year.

Finally, we looked at academics. First, we found that report card comments were strongly associated with letter grades in language and literature. After controlling for demographics, grade level, and attendance, students who received positive self-management, positive other SEL, positive preparedness, or positive academic comments averaged a B (higher than the average student grade, approximately a B–). Meanwhile, students who received a negative self-management, negative preparedness, or negative academic comment averaged in the C and C– ranges, which is up to a full letter grade lower than the average student.

Similarly, report card comments were strongly associated with letter grades in math. After controlling for demographics, grade level, and attendance, students who received a positive other SEL or positive preparedness comment averaged a B, and students who received a positive academic comment averaged a B+. Meanwhile, students who received a negative self-management, negative other SEL, or negative academic comment averaged a C, and those who received a negative preparedness comment averaged a C–. Thus, negative comments had two to three times greater an effect on letter grades than positive ones.

Our last set of analyses examined how report card comments were associated with standardized test scores. Only eleventh-graders were analyzed as only eleventh-graders had standardized test scores. Because standardized testing occurs toward the end of third quarter and is an accumulation of skills and knowledge, these analyses used comments and letter grades for quarters one, two, and three. Regression analyses using the comment categories were significant and able to explain 11% of the variation in standardized test scores for language and 16% of the variation in standardized test scores for math. While the effects of report card comments on standardized test scores were no longer significant after accounting for letter grades, this was not surprising in light of earlier analyses showing the strong behavior component in those grades.

Similar to our detailed examination of our letter grades analyses, we found that after controlling for modifiable factors, the initial effects of gender and ethnicity decreased by about 20% on language standardized test scores, and the initial effects of ethnicity were reduced by about 40% on math standardized test scores. (Gender never had a significant effect on math standardized test scores, so the modifiable factors could not reduce it further.)

In summary, the High School SEL-RCI Study was successful in discovering that report card comments were associated with fewer attendance problems, higher letter grades, and higher standardized test scores in a manner consistent with SEL theory. The finding that accounting for report card comments reduces academic disparities for gender and ethnicity has important implications in that targeting these modifiable factors may lead to greater educational equity.

THE ELEMENTARY SCHOOL SEL-RCI STUDY

The Elementary School SEL-RCI Study (Moceri & Elias, 2015) examined report cards from a suburban elementary school in Central New Jersey. This school had an enrollment of approximately 500 students with almost a third qualifying for a free or reduced lunch. Half of the students at this school were female, and about half of the students were black, Hispanic, Asian, or multiracial. The school provided us with report cards and school records for 186 fourth- and fifth-grade students from the 2007–2008 academic year.

Report cards for this school included behavioral comments, academic letter grades, and attendance variables. Comments and letter grades were provided for each quarter for each academic subject area: reading, writing, science, mathematics, and social studies. The school records included the students' grade level, special-needs status, and state standardized test scores. The race or ethnicity for individual students was not provided.

Teachers chose behavioral comments from a list of twenty-four possibilities. Unlike the other SEL-RCI studies, no limits were placed on the number of comments chosen. Similar to the High School SEL-RCI Study, no categories or groupings of the comments existed on the report card. We coded the comments to determine how well they matched the CASEL 5 conceptualization of SEL skills. A two-phase process determined that there were four major categories: self-management (e.g., works well independently or needs to pay closer attention in class), relationship skills (e.g., participates well in class discussions or needs to show more respect for others), academics/prepared/organized (e.g., brings materials to class daily or needs to complete homework regularly), and other (e.g., presents work neatly or conference requested by teacher). The first two were CASEL 5 skill areas, and the second two were not. Each of those four major categories had positive and negative categories. Three of the five CASEL 5 core competencies were not represented (i.e., self-awareness, social awareness, and responsible decision making).

As the Elementary SEL-RCI Study allowed teachers to choose up to twenty-four comments, we decided to use cluster analysis to see what types of comment groupings the teachers were naturalistically using, given their high degree of choice. This process revealed that teachers used the comments in one of three general ways, which we labeled the low, medium, and high clusters to describe them. Students in the low cluster were assigned a small number of positive comments (i.e., averaging less than two positive comments per class per quarter) and a small number of negative comments (i.e., averaging almost two negative comments per quarter). Students in the medium cluster were assigned a moderate number of positive comments (i.e., averaging almost six positive comments per class per quarter) and had a very small number of negative comments (i.e., averaging one negative comment per quarter). Finally, students in the high cluster were assigned many positive comments (i.e., averaging eight positive comments per class per quarter) and rarely had a negative comment (i.e., averaging less than one negative comment per quarter). Ambiguous comments were very rarely used, even in the low cluster.

We had strong findings when analyzing the relationship between comments and letter grades. In the first quarter, students in the low cluster averaged a B+, those in the medium cluster averaged an A–, and those in the high cluster averaged an A. In the fourth quarter, students in the low cluster averaged a B+, and those in the medium and high clusters averaged an A–. The above analyses controlled for gender, grade level, and attendance problems.

Next, we analyzed the effect of comment clusters on proficiency levels on standardized tests. The State of New Jersey designates students as partially proficient (PP), proficient (P), or advanced proficient (AP) separately for language (LA) and math (MA), based upon their performance on the New Jersey Assessment of Skills and Knowledge (NJASK), which was taken at the start of the fourth quarter. As less than 10% of the students at this school were PP, we recoded the proficiency levels for students to be designated as achieving AP or not (i.e., P and PP). Standardized test scores were only available for fourth-graders. We controlled for the effects of gender, attendance problems, and letter grades in the given subject area in the third quarter.

The analyses of the NJASK language scores only examined the medium and high clusters as none of the students in the low comment cluster group had AP status (a finding in itself). Students in the high positive-behaviors comments cluster were more likely to obtain AP on the LA NJASK than P or PP compared to students with medium positive-comments cluster. Surprisingly, the size of the effect was even stronger after controlling for concurrent letter grades.

The analyses of NJASK math scores were able to use all three clusters. Students with high positive-behaviors comments were more likely to obtain AP on the LA NJASK than P or PP compared to students with low positive-behaviors comments. However, the effect of comments on proficiency levels was no longer significant after controlling for letter grades.

In summary, the Elementary School SEL-RCI Study found strong evidence linking positive comments on the report card to better letter grades and some evidence linking positive comments to better standardized test performance. On average, students who received a medium or high number of positive comments on their report card received a third of a letter grade higher than those who received a low number of positive comments. Additionally, students who received more positive comments were more likely to achieve advanced proficiency on standardized tests. The findings applied to both "subjective" (i.e., language) and "objective" (i.e., mathematics) academic areas. But, once again, the comments were only partially able to assess the CASEL 5. Gender was not associated with academic performance in any of the above analyses.

OVERVIEW OF RESEARCH ON THE SEL-RCI

Overall, there was remarkable consistency among the Elementary School, Middle School, and High School SEL-RCI Studies (Kemp et al., 2015; Moceri & Elias, 2015; Moceri et al., 2015). This is especially impressive given that these studies were conducted at vastly different age levels, in different school districts, and with varying report card comment formats. Taken together, they revealed that students with more SEL skills, as represented by report card comments, had fewer attendance problems, higher letter grades, and better performance on standardized tests. These findings applied to both "subjective" (i.e., language) and "objective" (i.e., mathematics) academic areas. This is particularly impressive given that the comments were only partially able to assess the five core aspects of SEL (i.e., the CASEL 5). While these findings are highly positive, it was discouraging to see that black and Hispanic students, male students, and low-SES students tended to have worse academic outcomes (i.e., more negative comments, fewer positive comments, lower letter grades, and lower standardized test scores) than their white, female, and non-low-SES peers at the middle and high school levels. Yet, even with these expected but undesirable findings, it was encouraging to see that SEL-related skills measured by report card comments reduced these academic disparities for the demographic variables, and these factors are highly modifiable through SEL interventions. These findings provide a strong impetus for systematic assessment of SEL skills using the vehicle of report card comment sections, revised for this purpose.

RESOURCES

Utility: While it is beyond the scope of this Guide to provide comprehensive steps to improve student social-emotional and character competencies, there are resources that schools have used successfully to accomplish this goal. These are listed here, along with research specifically cited in this Guide.

Our guidelines have emerged from research and the ongoing practice of many schools that have pursued and continue to pursue social-emotional competencies, character virtues, and a positive school culture and climate. We include below: (a) some sources that you can continue to check to see examples and to find potential collaborators or mentors, (b) key sources of updated information on research findings, and (c) books to provide background on SEL and character virtues and guidance for the implementation of SEL and character interventions in schools and districts.

SEL AND CHARACTER EXAMPLES AND COLLABORATORS

- www.edutopia.org — Edutopia, the George Lucas Educational Foundation
- www.CASEL.org — CASEL, the Collaborative for Academic, Social, and Emotional Learning
- www.character.org — Character.org, formerly known as the Character Education Partnership, and Coordinator of National Schools of Character Awards
- www.schoolclimate.org — National School Climate Center
- www.characterandcitizenship.org — Center for Character and Citizenship
- www.jubileecentre.ac.uk — Jubilee Centre for Character and Virtue
- www.amenetwork.org — Association for Moral Education
- www.cfchildren.org — Committee for Children
- www.parenttoolkit.com/index.cfm?objectid=50A8EC10-32D8-11E4-B03B0050569A5318 — Parent Toolkit, created and maintained by NBC News Education Nation, providing developmental guidance on SEL in English and Spanish
- njasecd.org — New Jersey Alliance for Social, Emotional and Character Development
- sel.cse.edu — SEL Academy provides online courses and certificate programs in school-focused coordination and leadership of SEL, character, and related approaches (for school and district leaders and leadership teams) and direct instruction of SEL, character, and related approaches in classrooms, small groups, and after-school settings (for teachers, school support personnel, and after-school program providers) (sel.rutgers.edu)

STATE STANDARDS WITH SEL AND CHARACTER

- Kansas Social, Emotional, and Character Development Standards—http://www.character.org/wp-content/uploads/Kansas-Social-Emotional-Character-Dev-Standards.pdf
- Pennsylvania Standards for Student Interpersonal Skills—http://www.episcenter.psu.edu/sites/default/files/Student_Interpersonal_Skills_Standards.pdf
- Illinois Learning Standards: Social/Emotional Learning—http://www.isbe.net/ils/social_emotional/standards.htm
- CASEL Scan of State Learning Standards to Advance Social and Emotional Learning—https://www.casel.org/s/state-learning-standards-to-advance-social-and-emotional-learning.pdf

LIKERT RATING SYSTEM FOR SECD ADOPTED STATEWIDE

Kansas State Department of Education

- http://www.ksde.org/Agency/DivisionofLearningServices/CareerStandardsandAssessmentServices/ContentAreaM-Z/SchoolCounseling/Social,Emotional,andCharacterDevelopment.aspx
- http://www.ksde.org/Portals/0/CSAS/Content%20Area%20(M-Z)/School%20Counseling/Soc_Emot_Char_Dev/Likert%20Scale%20for%20SECD%20Student%20Growth%20Measure.pdf

Primary Ongoing Research References

- http://www.casel.org/library/building-academic-success-on-social-and-emotional-learning
- http://www.casel.org/library/2014/1/29/meta-analysis-of-school-based-universal-interventions
- https://characterandcitizenship.org/home-cerch

BOOKS FOR BACKGROUND ON AND IMPLEMENTATION OF SEL AND CHARACTER DEVELOPMENT

Background

- *Lessons From the Classroom* by Hal Urban
- *Character Matters* by Tom Lickona
- *You Can't Teach Through a Rat* by Marvin W. Berkowitz
- *Eight Habits of the Heart for Educators* by Clifton Taulbert

- *Relationships + Rules + Routines = Results* by Philip Vincent and Doug Grove
- *An Ethic of Excellence* by Ron Berger
- *Building Academic Success on Social-Emotional Learning: What Does the Research Say?* by Joe Zins and Colleagues
- *Emotionally Intelligent Parenting* by Maurice Elias, Steven Tobias, and Brian Friedlander

Implementation of SEL and Character Development

- *Handbook of Social and Emotional Learning: Research and Practice* edited by Joseph A. Durlak, Celene E. Domitrovich, Roger P. Weissberg, and Thomas P. Gullotta
- *Promoting Social and Emotional Learning: Guidelines for Educators* by Maurice Elias, Joe Zins, et al.
- *Building Learning Communities With Character* by Bernard Novick, Jeffrey S. Kress, and Maurice Elias
- *Building an Intentional School Culture* by Charles Elbot and David Fulton
- *The Educators' Guide to Emotional Intelligence: Social-Emotional Learning in the Classroom* edited by Maurice Elias and Harriett Arnold
- *Transforming School Leadership and Management to Support Student Learning and Development: The Field Guide to Comer Schools in Action* by Edward T. Joyner, Michael Ben-Avie, and James P. Comer
- *The School Leader's Guide to Student Learning Supports: New Directions for Addressing Barriers to Learning* by Howard S. Adelman and Linda Taylor
- *Smart and Good High Schools* by Thomas Lickona and Matthew Davidson
- *Schools of Social-Emotional Competence and Character: Actions for School Leaders, Teachers, and School Support Professionals* by Maurice Elias and Marvin Berkowitz

REFERENCES

Beland, K. (Ed.). (2003). *Eleven principles sourcebook*. Washington, DC: Character Education Partnership.

Brown, P. M., Corrigan, M. W., & Higgins-D'Alessandro, A. (Eds.). (2012). *The handbook of prosocial education*. Lanham, MD: Rowman & Littlefield.

Collaborative for Academic, Social, and Emotional Learning. (2003). *Safe and sound: An education leader's guide to evidence-based social and emotional learning (SEL) programs*. Chicago, IL: Author.

Dunkelblau, E. (2009). *Social-emotional and character development: A laminated resource card for teachers, for students, for parents*. Port Chester, NY: National Professional Resources.

Durlak, J. A., Domitrovich, C., Weissberg, R. P., & Gullotta, T. P. (Eds.). (2015). *Handbook of social and emotional learning (SEL): Research and practice*. New York, NY: Guilford.

Elias, M. J., & Arnold, H. A. (Eds.). (2006). *The educator's guide to emotional intelligence and academic achievement: Social-emotional learning in the classroom*. Thousand Oaks, CA: Corwin.

Elias, M. J., & Berkowitz, M. (2016). *Schools of social-emotional competence and character: Actions for school leaders, teachers, and school support professionals* [Laminated resource card]. Port Chester, NY: National Professional Resources.

Elias, M. J., Zins, J. E., Weissberg, R. P., Frey, K., Greenberg, M., Haynes, N., . . . Shriver, T. (1997). *Promoting social and emotional learning: Guidelines for educators*. Alexandria, VA: Association for Supervision and Curriculum Development.

Friedman, S. J., & Frisbie, D. A. (1995). The influence of report cards on the validity of grades reported to parents. *Educational & Psychological Measurement, 55*, 5–26.

Friedman, S. J., Valde, G. A., & Obermeyer, B. J. (1998). Computerized report card comment menus: Teacher use and teacher parent perceptions. *Spectrum, 16*, 37–42.

Kemp, S. N., Moceri, D. C., & Elias, M. J. (2015). Minority disproportionality in general education. (Journal article under review.)

Moceri, D. C., & Elias, M. J. (2015). Grading the other side of the report card: How comments on an elementary school's report card are connected to current and future academic performance. (Journal article under review.)

Moceri, D. C., Elias, M. J., Fishman, D. B., Epstein, Y., & Selby, E. A. (2015). Social-emotional competencies and academic achievement in diverse high school youth. (Journal article under review.)

Nucci, L., Narvaez, D., & Krettenauer, T. (Eds.). (2014). *Handbook of moral and character education* (2nd ed.). New York, NY: Routledge.

Payton, J., Weissberg, R. P., Durlak, J. A., Dymnicki, A. B., Taylor, R. D., Schellinger, K. B., & Pachan, M. (2008). *The positive impact of social and emotional learning for kindergarten to eighth-grade students: Findings from three scientific reviews*. Chicago, IL: Collaborative for Academic, Social, and Emotional Learning.

Tough, P. (2012). *How students succeed: Grit, curiosity and the hidden power of character*. New York, NY: Houghton Mifflin Harcourt.

A SAGE Company

CORWIN HAS ONE MISSION: to enhance education through intentional professional learning.

We build long-term relationships with our authors, educators, clients, and associations who partner with us to develop and continuously improve the best evidence-based practices that establish and support lifelong learning.

Solutions you want. Experts you trust. Results you need.